cational Administration

L E C T I O N O F C A S E S T U D I E S

t E. Kirschmann
·γ of Bridgeport

Merrill,
an imprint of Prentice Hall
Upper Saddle River, New Jersey 07458

Library of Congress Cataloging–in–Publication Data

Kirschmann, Robert E.
    Educational administration : a collection of case studies / by Robert E. Kirschmann.
      p. cm.
    Includes bibliographical references and index.
    ISBN 0-13-352635-6 (pbk. : alk. paper)
    1. School management and organization–United States–Case studies.   I. Title.
LB2805.K518   1996
371'.00973–dc20   95–10755
                                                                        CIP

Editor: Debra A. Stollenwerk
Production Editor: Alexandrina Benedicto Wolf
Design Coordinator: Jill E. Bonar
Text Designer: Matthew Williams
Cover Designer: Rod Harris
Production Manager: Patricia A. Tonneman
Electronic Text Management: Marilyn Wilson Phelps, Matthew Williams, Karen L. Bretz,
    Tracey B. Ward

This book was set in Nofret and Futura by Prentice Hall and was printed and bound by
Quebecor Printing/Book Press. The cover was printed by Phoenix Color Corp.

© 1996 by Prentice-Hall, Inc.
A Pearson Education Company
Upper Saddle River, NJ 07458

Printed in the United States of America

10 9 8 7 6 5 4 3 2 1

ISBN: 0-13-352635-6

Prentice-Hall International (UK) Limited,London
Prentice-Hall of Australia Pty. Limited, Sydney
Prentice-Hall Canada Inc., Toronto
Prentice-Hall Hispanoamericana, S.A., Mexico
Prentice-Hall of India Private Limited, New Delhi
Prentice-Hall of Japan, Inc., Tokyo
Pearson Education Asia Pte. Ltd., Singapore
Editora Prentice-Hall do Brasil, Ltda., Rio de Janeiro

To the loving memory of

Robert E. Kirschmann, Sr., and Mary P. Wright

Preface

• • • • • •

This is a casebook intended to provide the learner with a look into the problems confronting administrators at all levels and in a variety of settings. It is designed to be used either as a companion text for a great variety of courses or as the primary focus of a workshop or in-service training program for practicing educators or administrators. Some generic names of courses for which it would be appropriate are as follows:

1. Introduction to Administration
2. The Principalship
3. Supervision
4. School Law
5. Issues and Problems in Education
6. Problem Solving for Educators and Administrators
7. Central Office Administration

The book is designed to provide both experienced administrators and those not yet initiated with an opportunity to review theory by applying it to the situations presented. More important, as students go through the cases in this book, they will have an opportunity to examine their assumptions, beliefs, values, and style. It is essential that all professionals revitalize themselves by a periodic and systematic in-depth look inward. In addition, these cases will afford the occasion to sharpen decision-making skills, analyze the process by which decisions are made, and focus on legal, ethical, and career-altering issues. The press of problems the administrator must handle on a daily basis usually precludes systematic review or a detached perspective.

When the cases presented in the following chapters are discussed in a class or workshop setting, learners should have the opportunity to validate, modify, or critique their own and their colleagues' performances. One of the greatest problems facing administrators is isolation. In practice it is seldom possible and is not always advisable to discuss problems and your reaction to them with colleagues. The assumption in some districts is that educators who seek to discuss the situations they face, except in the form of an occasional complaint, are weak or incompetent. In a classroom setting such exchanges have very little risk and can provide valuable feedback.

Most cases presented in this book are based on situations that I have encountered as an administrator or that have confronted my administrator colleagues. The specifics have been altered to protect the actual parties involved, and in some instances several similar incidents have been consolidated into one case. I have done my best to retain the flavor of the actual events by reporting them in the informal language and the chronology in which they were made known to the administrator to whom they were originally presented. A few of the cases are based on speculation about what would have happened if a real situation had an unexpected twist or if some outside factor had intervened. I find it interesting to note that the cases whose authenticity my students have challenged were always genuine.

Often, at the conclusion of the discussion of a case, the participants want to know what really happened. The danger of disclosing the actual outcome is that it becomes too easy to assume either that the particular outcome was inevitable or that it is the best possible solution to the problem. A resolution that may be desirable and practical in one situation may not work in very similar circumstances at a different time or place or with different participants. The cases presented are open-ended on purpose, and, as in real life, students can never be certain when they reach a final decision whether the resolutions they have devised are the best possible ones. The important thing is that they examine the situations, dissect the issues, and evaluate alternatives until they feel that their solutions are sound, ethical, and viable. There may be several legitimate paths to a positive outcome, or there may only be a choice among evils.

Many of the cases presented, especially in the first two chapters, are routine and fairly mundane. It is my belief that the vast bulk of decisions administrators make are in that vein. The more dramatic cases get attention and may have serious consequences personally and professionally, but I believe that the quality of leadership lies more surely in the daily exercise of judgment than in the resolution of high-visibility issues.

To gain the most from these cases, learners must place themselves as completely as possible into the role described. It may be far more difficult for a person currently serving as a superintendent or a high school principal to project himself or herself into the position of an elementary principal than it is for someone who has no administrative experience. I have frequently found that the solutions reached by a given person when assuming one role are significantly different from the solutions found by that same person when assuming a different role. I hope the cases presented will prove interesting.

ABOUT THE BOOK'S ORGANIZATION AND FEATURES

This book has several features I would like to highlight. When using cases in my classes, I have found that it is sometimes difficult to select a scenario that is germane to the topic at hand. That is, in fact, why I began to develop many of the cases in this book. For your convenience, I have categorized the cases in four different ways. First, I have organized the chapters so that the first 13 cases concern elementary school, the next 13 middle school, the following 14 high school, and the last 10 the central office.

The second form of organization is in the last half of the titles of the problems. The titles were designed to suggest what the focus of the case might be. Since cases, especially the more complex ones, may be categorized in many different ways, at the beginning of the book I have placed a **topic matrix**. The matrix classifies the cases in a different way from the chapter organization or the case titles. At the end of the book is an index, which presents yet another way of viewing them. Although there are many other possible ways of grouping, these four types of classification should assist in the selection of the cases appropriate at a given juncture. The cases may be used in any order and for a wide variety of purposes.

I present a specific **setting** at the beginning of each chapter. All the cases in the chapter are written with that particular setting in mind. None of the individual cases have background material within them. Thus, the instructor can easily change or ignore the setting or can refer the students to the background material at the beginning of the chapter.

Similarly, in the **chapter summary**, I briefly discuss the nature of the setting presented and the roles the students were to assume when responding to the problems. By detaching this material from the cases themselves, I intend to give the instructor the flexibility to use or ignore the material or to have students read the material before or after they tackle the cases. The same is true of the **summary questions**, which follow the chapter summary in each chapter.

After the questions for each case, there is a **suggested activity**. Some of the activities require students to do research or get legal opinions. Others require the writing of position papers, letters, newspaper articles, or chronicles of events. The variety of those activities and the involvement they require are designed to make the cases more than simple intellectual exercises.

The **suggested reading** list at the end of each chapter is designed to give the learner a start in exploring the issues more completely.

A WORD ABOUT CASE STUDY METHODOLOGY

The case study approach is a very flexible method that is especially useful in developing skills, examining the affective domain, looking at process, and examining personal style and values. It can be used to teach even young children if the cases are short and simple. The content and complexity of the cases should be correlated to the maturity and experience level of the students and the specific purposes of the instructor.

The advantages of the case study approach are as follows:

1. Students can be given the same material in the same manner at the same time and therefore have a common basis for discussing, analyzing, and finding solutions to the situations presented.
2. Students who have not had a particular type of experience can be exposed to the problems and situations typical of the situation.
3. Since no real actions are taken in response to a case study, it is a low-risk learning technique.
4. Case studies can help students see familiar situations from a new perspective.

5. If students are not satisfied with the solutions presented to a given problem, they can start the process over entirely or go back to whatever point in the case they wish.
6. Students can look back at the text if they need to verify some point.
7. Although students may disagree on how to interpret the information given, the information itself remains a constant.
8. In a case study format, students may resolve a problem by applying one administrative theory or problem-solving approach and then resolve the same problem again using different assumptions. Thus they can compare and contrast theories and techniques in a systematic way.
9. Case studies provide an opportunity for students to dissect their approaches and examine their decision-making skills.
10. Case studies give students an opportunity to try out various approaches they might not otherwise consider.
11. Case studies can be used to help students translate theory into practice.
12. Case studies give students a chance to honestly examine their personal value systems and prejudices.
13. Students and instructors can use a case in whatever way best suits their purposes.
14. Cases may be used as a means of either formative or summative evaluation.
15. Because case studies involve substantial student participation, they are an effective means of keeping students actively involved in a lesson. The research on adult learning styles indicates that adults need to be presented with a variety of teaching techniques in order to receive the maximum advantage from instruction. Case studies are a good balance to lectures and discussions of abstract principles.

Case study methodology obviously has its limitations as well:

1. Once students have determined the action they would take at a given point, they have no way of seeing the results of their decision. This is especially problematic in cases with several stages. To continue the case, the author must assume that a certain course of action has been taken. The students' decisions might have been to select a very different response, which would then alter everything that follows.
2. Before the problem ever presented itself, the student might have taken steps that would have altered the situation substantially or eliminated the problem entirely.
3. The students cannot acquire additional information about the case or the setting, beyond what is presented, unless the students or the instructor generate that information.
4. Cases sometimes seem to have been explored exhaustively when in fact additional concerns really need to be considered. In actual practice, unconsidered options sometimes make themselves apparent.
5. Cases are presented as neat entities unto themselves. In reality all administrators are faced with such situations while they are in the midst of dealing

with any number of other concurrent concerns, all of which may be demanding immediate attention.

6. The value of the cases depends to some extent on the ability of the students to project themselves into the situation. Case study methodology is most useful in developing skills and in the affective domain. If students approach cases from a very cognitive orientation, much of the potential value of the methodology will be lost.

Instructors can and have used cases in any number of ways. Cases usually do not lend themselves well to individual independent study. Whether students initially respond to the cases independently, in small groups, or as an entire class, it is most often during the debriefing, critiquing, debating, or some other exchange of views that the most valuable learning takes place. We seem to need other people to validate or disagree with our solutions and to give us other forms of stimulation and feedback if we are going to obtain maximum benefit from this instructional technique.

Case study theory and method and decision-making techniques will not be explored in great depth is this book. The following references, however, can provide the learner with a broad understanding of both these tools.

SUGGESTED READING

Anderson, D. R. (1982). *An introduction to management science: Quantitative approaches to decision making.* St. Paul, MN: West.

Clare, V. N. (1986). The effectiveness of case studies in training principals: Using the deliberative orientation. *Peabody Journal of Education, 63*(1), 187–195.

Dubin, A. E. (1987). Administrative training: Socializing our school leaders. *Planning and Change, 18*(1), 33–37.

Fielder, F. E. (1984). *Improving leadership effectiveness: The leader match concept.* New York: Wiley.

Florio-Ruane, S., & Clark, C. M. (1990). Using case studies to enrich field experience. *Teacher Education Quarterly, 18*(1), 17–28.

Gorton, R. A. (1987). *School leadership and administration: Important concepts, case studies and simulations.* Dubuque, IA: W. C. Brown.

Herzberg, F. (1976). *The managerial choice: To be efficient and to be human.* Homewood, IL: Dow Jones-Irwin.

Hoy, W. K. (1978). *Educational administration: Theory, research, and practice.* New York: Random House.

Hudspeth, D., & Knirk, F. G. (1989). Case study materials: Strategies for design and use. *Performance Improvement Quarterly, 2*(4), 30–41.

Lakomski, G. (1987). Case study methodology and the rational management of interaction. *Educational management and administration, 15*(2), 147–157.

Pennings, J. M. (1983). *Decision making: An organizational behavior approach.* New York: M. Wiener.

Plunkett, L. C. (1982). *The proactive manager: The complete book of problem solving and decision making*. New York: Wiley.

Romm, T., & Mahler, S. (1991). The case study challenge: A new approach to an old method. *Management Education and Development, 22*(4), 292–301.

Sample, J. (1983, February). The Vroom and Yetton normative leadership model applied to public school case examples. Paper presented at the quarterly meeting of the School Improvement Network (SINET), Gainesville, FL. (Can be obtained through ERIC.)

Vroom, V. H. (1988). *The new leadership: Managing participation in organizations*. Englewood Cliffs, NJ: Prentice Hall.

Wasserman, S. (1993). *Getting down to cases: Learning to teach with case studies*. New York: Teachers College Press.

Additional references for material on decision making may be found at the end of each chapter.

STEREOTYPING

When preparing these cases, I originally tried to eliminate all racial, ethnic, and gender references and descriptors that might provide the basis for potential bias. I found that my cases lacked reality because I had stripped the people I was describing of all human characteristics. People have gender and race. We belong to various ethnic groups, have socioeconomic status, and wear glasses, contact lenses, or neither. We are relatively tall or short, fat or thin, well educated or not, socially adept or not, clean or dirty, appropriately or inappropriately dressed, pleasant or obnoxious, sophisticated or crude, and so on. As administrators, we must deal with people who sometimes reinforce negative stereotypes or who may seem to be in the right by virtue of appearing to fit some image we carry of a good person.

Because we are human, we have preconceived notions that we cannot rid ourselves of completely. We all have biases. We all react to first impressions. I have returned some of the human characteristics to the people described in the cases because we must learn to acknowledge our prejudices and not allow them to dictate our actions or cloud our thinking.

By far the most extreme stereotype in these cases is the male chauvinist football coach. It is easy to overlook this sort of stereotype because male football coaches are not protected by the guardians of the politically correct. The chauvinist coach is such a strong stereotype that we accept the image without question. Throughout this book you must be aware of your responsibility to respond to what people do and say, not to any classification they may fit. It is important to acknowledge that, although one of the male coaches in this collection of cases is a chauvinist, there is no reason to suspect that the others described are. Treat each individual depicted according to the information you have about him or her, not according to assumed character traits.

ACKNOWLEDGMENT

I hereby gratefully acknowledge all the help, encouragement, support, and sacrifice given me by my wife, Kathleen, my son, Rob, and my daughter, Mary, during the writing of this book.

I take this opportunity to thank my colleagues and students for their encouragement. I appreciate the invaluable feedback from the following reviewers: H. Prentice Baptiste, Kansas State University; Larry W. Hughes, University of Houston; Robert E. Millward, Indiana University of Pennsylvania; Cynthia J. Norris, University of Houston; Kent Peterson, University of Wisconsin-Madison; Ulrich C. Reitzug, University of Wisconsin-Milwaukee; James Scheurich, University of Texas-Austin; Carol Cook Schunk, Independent Educational Consultant; and Frederick C. Wendel, University of Nebraska-Lincoln. I am also indebted to all the editors at Prentice Hall with whom I have worked, especially Debbie Stollenwerk.

Robert E. Kirschmann

Contents

· · · · · ·

CHAPTER 3   **THE DAILY PROBLEMS OF A HIGH SCHOOL
PRINCIPAL   57**

CHAPTER 4   **DAILY PROBLEMS OF THE CENTRAL OFFICE**   **99**

1

......

The Daily Problems of an Elementary School Principal

BACKGROUND

For all the situations presented in this chapter, assume that you are the principal and sole building administrator of a 550-student K–6 elementary school in a community that was once rural but is now becoming increasingly suburban. There is some friction between the very stable population of people who have lived in the community all their lives and the newcomers. The newly arrived residents have different values and aspirations from the established residents. The population moving in is more politically active and more demanding of the school system.

Two years ago there was a hotly contested school board election, and four of the seven seats are now held by nonnatives. Since then, most school board votes have been 4–3 splits. The previous principal felt very pressured by the bickering of the school board and took early retirement.

You were hired last year by a vote that was reported to be unanimous but in reality was another 4–3 split. You did not know that the vote was split until you had been on the job for two months. The other finalist had grown up in the community. You came in from a neighboring state and were not familiar with the area. The faculty members were divided as to which of the two finalists they wanted for their principal. It took most of your first year to establish yourself firmly in your position, but now you have the bulk of the staff behind you. You were hired with the understanding that you would upgrade the curriculum and the academic standards.

PROBLEM 1—THE RIDICULED CHILD: THE SOCIAL PROBLEMS OF A PARENT AND CHILD

A very angry woman has barged into your office moments before the beginning of the school day. She abruptly introduces herself as Mrs. Shelby, the mother of Brenda, an unpleasant and unpopular fourth-grade girl. You are vaguely aware that Brenda is often the brunt of rather cruel taunts by the other children. She is abrasive and disruptive in class and is not strong academically.

The mother tells you that her daughter came home crying for the third day in a row because the kids had made fun of her and refused to allow her to play with them. The most offensive of all is a girl named Dawn, who ridicules Brenda constantly and gets the other children to make fun of Brenda as well.

Mrs. Shelby says she called Brenda's teacher, Mrs. Nash, last Friday, and Mrs. Nash said she would speak to Dawn. When Brenda came home from school on Monday, she told her mother that Dawn had been as mean to her as ever.

Last night Mrs. Shelby called Mrs. Nash again. Mrs. Nash said that she had spoken to Dawn and that the child had said she would be nice to Brenda even though she didn't like her. Mrs. Nash said there was nothing more she could do. If she tried to shield Brenda from all ridicule, Brenda would become dependent on her and even less able to form positive relationships with her classmates. Mrs. Nash said that one girl, Carol, had tried to make friends with Brenda but that

Brenda had rejected her. Mrs. Nash said that she could not make children like each other and that, as long as no one physically hurt Brenda or made fun of her in class, there was nothing more she could do.

Mrs. Shelby says she was so angry when she heard what Mrs. Nash had to say, she slammed down the receiver and decided to come in to see you to make sure that the ridicule is stopped.

Case Questions

1. What do you feel is the proper way to handle people who storm into your office without appointments?
2. Once this matter is brought to your attention, is there anything more you feel you must find out before taking any action?
3. Do you feel Mrs. Nash acted appropriately? Why or why not?
4. Now that you have been confronted with this problem, how do you respond?
5. How would you choose in general to deal with children who ridiculed others? With the victims of ridicule?
6. How would you choose in general to deal with irate parents?

SUGGESTED ACTIVITY: Write a short opinion paper discussing what responsibility schools should have for the development of students' social skills. If you believe schools have such a responsibility, outline the steps by which a curriculum could be established to meet that responsibility.

PROBLEM 2—DISTRIBUTION OF SUPPLIES: INTRASTAFF FRICTION

Greg Uland, sixth-grade teacher, has come into your office after school, quite annoyed. He says that he has just gone into the supply closet to get $8\frac{1}{2}$ x 11-inch white lined paper for his students to write final copies of their essays for a contest. The essays must be turned in tomorrow. His students have been working on the essays for nearly two weeks and expect to have them submitted. The contest rules say that the essays must be submitted on $8\frac{1}{2}$ x 11-inch white lined paper. There is none in the supply closet, and the year isn't even half over.

He says that the reason the paper is gone is that other teachers have taken it all and hidden it away in their rooms. The worst offenders, according to Greg, are Marina Pulaski and Sharon Massi. Uland claims that the former principal had always allowed the two of them to have whatever they wanted, even if it meant that other people had to do without.

You know that you ordered 10% more of all paper supplies than had been ordered the previous year, because several teachers had complained that the supplies had run out before the end of the year. In addition, the student population has been rising slowly but steadily.

You go down to the supply closet with Greg and find that he is right: All the 8½ x 11-inch white lined paper is gone. You cannot imagine that two teachers could possibly have stockpiled enough paper to exhaust the supply this early in the year.

You tell Greg that you'll get the necessary paper for him by tomorrow. After he leaves, you go to Marina Pulaski's room and politely ask if she has any 8½ x 11-inch white lined paper. The pleasant look with which she greeted you disappears, and she says that she has two unopened reams and a small quantity left of another ream. She invites you to search her room if you think she has some huge stockpile hidden somewhere. You say that won't be necessary, but you ask if you may borrow one ream, promising to replace it. She hands you the paper in silence.

Case Questions

1. What do you suspect is going on here?
2. Are there problems with the professional relationships in your building–problems with which you need to become involved? If so, what do you do?
3. How can you tell if there is unproductive tension among staff members?
4. Your supply budget for the year has been expended. What do you do about the shortage of 8½ x 11-inch white lined paper?
5. How do you go about ordering supplies for next year?
6. How do you monitor what has been happening to your supplies?
7. What can you do to ensure an equitable distribution of supplies in the future?
8. What else, if anything, do you need to know to deal effectively with this situation?

SUGGESTED ACTIVITY: Describe how you know when someone is attempting to manipulate you, and discuss strategies to counteract such manipulation.

PROBLEM 3—SCHEDULING: INTEGRATING NEW PERSONNEL INTO A SCHOOL

Until recently, each classroom teacher was responsible for teaching art, music, and health to his or her classes. Teachers at the fourth- and sixth-grade levels had decided among themselves to divide up those responsibilities and to exchange classes for those subjects. That arrangement was approved by the previous administration. The quality of instruction and the amount of time spent on art, music, and health varied tremendously from classroom to classroom.

The new members of the school board voted to add two new positions to the faculty, an art teacher and a music teacher. The school population had increased by more than 40 pupils, and there was general agreement that the school needed additional staff. Many people thought another classroom teacher should be added and the faculty lounge should be turned into a classroom. There have been three classes at every grade level, but first grade is the largest group going through the school, and those people wanted to create a fourth second-grade class for next year. That idea was rejected in favor of hiring an art teacher and a music teacher, and increasing the school nurse from half time to full time. Half of the nurse's responsibilities would be to teach health.

You must develop a schedule for next year. Each class must be served by the art teacher, the music teacher, and the nurse, who is to teach health. The school has long had a full-time elementary gym teacher.

By contract each teacher, including the nurse, the librarian, and the art, music, and physical education teachers, must have one-half hour for lunch each day and a total of two hours of preparation time per week. You must provide coverage for bus students for one-half hour before and after school, and supervision for students during recess and lunch. Those duties must be evenly distributed.

You have full-day kindergarten. Your classes begin at 8:45 A.M. and school is dismissed at 3:00 P.M. There are approximately 25 students per class, except in the first grade, which has 29 per class. The school year is 38 weeks long.

Your staff for next year is as follows:

Kindergarten: Paula Ableson, Maddie Baker, and Faith Clark
First Grade: Harriet Davis, Laura Eldridge, and Martha Feinstein
Second Grade: Elizabeth Grant, Karen Holt, and Tricia Ingles
Third Grade: Sandra Johnson, Terri Kennedy, and Maria Lopez
Fourth Grade: Sharon Massi, Harriet Nash, and Ruth Obanski
Fifth Grade: Marina Pulaski, Marion Quinn, and Steve Roth
Sixth Grade: Pat Smith, Diane Taylor, and Greg Uland
Music: Andy Valentine
Art: Ruthann Wagner
Physical Education: Fred Xenon
Nurse: Karin Young
Special Education: Tanya Zimmerman and Mary Zapara
Librarian: Lillian Bechtold

Note: The special-education teachers have a pull-out program and arrange their own schedules. Each is responsible, however, for her share of bus, lunch, and playground duty, as is the librarian.

You must arrange a weekly master schedule so that all students receive an equal amount of instruction in art, music, physical education, and health, all duties are adequately covered, and each teacher has a free lunch period between 11:30 and 1:00 daily and two hours of preparation time per week. Provide a yearly schedule for duties, dividing them as fairly as possible.

Case Questions

1. What process did you use to develop your schedule?
2. Would you involve the faculty in drawing up the schedule? Why or why not?
3. Before you make your schedule final, how will you test it to make sure it meets all the requirements?
4. How will you handle faculty concerns, both before the schedule is drawn up and after it is presented?

SUGGESTED ACTIVITY: Seek out three references on elementary-school scheduling.

PROBLEM 4—ESTABLISHING A DISCIPLINE POLICY: DEVELOPING A PROCESS FOR MAKING SIGNIFICANT DECISIONS

In the past, each teacher established her or his own policy regarding discipline. The past principal insisted that if a teacher sent a student to the office, a second student had to be sent shortly after with a note from the teacher describing the offense. Once a teacher made a discipline referral, that teacher was expected to accept whatever decision the principal made concerning the infraction. If the principal had some concern about the way a teacher was handling discipline, the principal spoke privately to the teacher.

The school board established a discipline code for the junior-senior high school at the insistence of that school's principal, but it made no specific provision for discipline at the elementary level. An elementary discipline policy had been established at some point in the distant past, but it simply established the penalties for infractions such as chewing gum, running in the halls, talking in line, fighting on the playground, and tardiness. That policy has fallen into disuse.

The new school board, by a 4–3 vote, has given the elementary school two months to come up with a discipline policy. As the principal, you have been instructed to establish a committee consisting of teachers and parents, with you as its chair, to write a discipline policy for your school. That policy is to be presented to the board for its approval. Furthermore, you have been instructed to look at *Assertive Discipline* as a possible approach to schoolwide discipline.

Case Questions

1. How do you go about complying with the school board's request?
2. How will you present the policy to the school board?
3. What key things do you want in a discipline policy?

SUGGESTED ACTIVITY: Find out the legal guidelines for discipline policies in your state.

PROBLEM 5—HEAD LICE:
ELIMINATING INFESTATION WHILE MINIMIZING DISRUPTION

Karin Young, the school nurse, has come into your office and told you that she has found head lice on Brooke Wilson, a second-grader. Karin informs you that Brooke had lice last year as well. Karin has checked Brooke's brother Paul, in kindergarten, and found that he has head lice, too.

School policy is that any child with head lice must be excluded from school until the lice are eliminated. Karin has a pamphlet ready to give Mrs. Wilson that explains how to get rid of head lice. Both children are in the nurse's office, and Karin is trying to get in touch with their mother to have her come and take them home. There is no answer either at home or at the emergency number listed on the children's health card. Brooke is crying and has been since the lice were discovered.

Karin has searched the heads of all the other students in Brooke's room and has not found any other infected children. She now wants to inspect the heads of all the kindergarteners. Karin hopes that she has caught the problem before the infestation had a chance to spread. She tells you that the last time Brooke Wilson brought lice to school, nearly a quarter of the primary-grade students were infected.

The Wilsons are longtime residents of the community, and several of the parents who had moved in recently complained bitterly the last time they found that their children had head lice. Many people said that the school should be responsible for providing the special shampoo to kill the lice and detergents for washing all the clothing, bedding, and plush surfaces their children's heads may have touched.

Karin wants your permission to send letters home to the parents of all children in kindergarten, first grade, and second grade, telling them that head lice have been found, asking them to check their children's heads, notifying them that their children should not be sent to school if they have lice, and giving instructions as to how to check for the lice and eliminate them. She says that last year she had to meet all the primary-grade children at the door and examine their heads to make sure they were free of lice. It was not a pleasant duty, and she would like to avoid doing it again.

Case Questions

1. Do you have the nurse check the heads of all the kindergarten students? Why or why not?

2. Do you have the nurse send the notice home to all primary-grade parents? Why or why not?

3. What, if anything, do you do about the two Wilson children in the nurse's office?

4. Do you have the nurse do spot checks of primary-grade children for the next several days to monitor them for infestation?

5. How can you prepare for any parent inquiries?

6. What do you do when you cannot reach parents at the numbers listed on the student emergency cards?

SUGGESTED ACTIVITY: Develop guidelines for minimizing the spread of contagious diseases and parasites among primary-grade children.

PROBLEM 6—BILLY: DEALING WITH A BULLY

Harriet Nash, fourth-grade teacher, has been having more and more trouble with Billy Osborn. Billy has always been big for his age and, against your better judgment, was kept back this past year. He is loud and obnoxious and is a bully. The last time he was sent to your office, he burst into tears as soon as you asked him what had happened. It took you several minutes to get him quieted down. You assigned him four nights of detention for being disruptive in class. By the time he left your office, he had the wise-guy look on his face that has become his trademark.

You know that Harriet does not have much patience in general and that she has had difficulty dealing with Billy since the beginning of the school year. She is not alone. The only teacher Billy has ever gotten along well with is Fred Xenon, the physical education teacher. Even the highly respected and loving Jane Richland, Billy's now-retired first-grade teacher, said Billy was just about the most exasperating child she had ever had. She felt that she had failed him.

Today Billy stuck out his tongue and swore at Harriet Nash. She is demanding that he be suspended from school. You feel that you have no choice but to suspend him.

You phone his mother, who says that she can't come and get him. He will just have to sit in the office until school is over and come home on the bus as usual. She says that no one can control Billy and that she has just about given up. She says that the only way she can make him obey at all is to give him a good sound spanking. He is now too big for her to spank, so she turns him over to Billy's stepfather, who does the job.

She tells you that she is giving you permission to strap him soundly. She will put it in writing. Spanking is prohibited by school board policy, and you inform Billy's mother that you will not spank him. She says that if you don't have the guts to handle the situation, you can't blame her if the kid runs all over you, and she hangs up the phone.

Case Questions

1. What do you do with Billy now?
2. What additional information, if any, do you need?
3. What long-range approach will you take with Billy?
4. How can you work with Harriet Nash to change Billy's behavior?

5. What approach will you take with Billy's mother?
6. Is there ample reason to investigate for child abuse?

SUGGESTED ACTIVITY: Examine the research on identifying and dealing with bullies.

PROBLEM 7—THE PROPOSED EXPANSION: DETERMINING THE BEST POSSIBLE EDUCATIONAL OUTCOME WHILE CONSIDERING COSTS

Your school was built in 1954 and was designed to accommodate 500 students. Originally it had a multipurpose room that served as a combination cafeteria, gym, and auditorium. In 1967 a new gym, with locker rooms, was added. That gym is used by the junior high students for basketball practice and home games, and by the community in the evenings. You use the gym for your physical education program, but your fifth-and-sixth-grade after-school basketball program still uses the cafeteria. In 1974 the library was nearly doubled in size and became a media center. In 1986 the playground facilities were expanded and improved. The building has been fairly well maintained, and the community takes pride in it.

Over the past five years, your school's student population has been growing steadily. The growth reflects both the influx of suburbanites and a slight rise in the birthrate. Current projections are for the population to continue to increase modestly for the next five years.

Four years ago several family farms were sold to developers. The developers planned to subdivide the land and build housing designed for the upper middle class. A local economic downturn delayed new construction, but recently several permits for new construction have been issued. The new construction permits are for more modest houses than were originally envisioned, but it appears likely that several hundred new houses will be constructed in the community over the next few years. If that happens, an increase of 150 elementary school students will be expected in the next five years. The population in grades 7–12 would increase by nearly the same number, but more slowly.

The entire community realizes that it must expand its school facilities. Rumors from the state capital indicate that state aid for new school construction will probably be decreased in the near future but that requests submitted quickly will be considered under the present formula, in which the state pays approximately 75% of the cost of new construction.

Four plans have been proposed concerning the elementary school. The first is to go to half-day kindergarten, to turn one of the present kindergarten rooms into a first grade room, to add another lunch wave to eliminate the need to expand the cafeteria, and to add five more classrooms, a storeroom, and student bathrooms by extending the main corridor. That would allow four classrooms at every grade level. This proposal also includes replacing the boiler with a more efficient model that could supply the required additional heat and hot water. This is the least expensive alternative, but it would delay any renovations of the high school until some later point.

Plan 2 is to leave your building as is and to build a new middle school for students in grades 5–8. The present junior-senior high school would house grades 9–12 and would not be physically altered. This is the most expensive alternative.

Plan 3 is to build a K–1 building on your campus. The new building would be a self-contained facility. You would be principal of both buildings, but an assistant principal would be hired and would have primary responsibility for the new building. The high school would remain 7–12 but would undergo a modest expansion at a later date. The present high school was designed to house 500 students and is nearly at capacity now. This is the second least expensive option.

Plan 4 is to build another elementary school in the area of the projected new development. If that happened, the majority of new families would attend that school, and your school would serve primarily the established residents. The superintendent's office, a converted old school in the middle of the village, would be sold as commercial property, one wing of your building would be converted into the new superintendent's office, and you would have approximately 300–350 students, with two classrooms at every level. The high school would remain 7–12, but would have an additional classroom wing added. When the income anticipated from the sale of the present central office building is factored in, this is the second most expensive plan.

The school board has decided to select one of these plans within the next three months so that they can hire an architect and submit the plans to the state before the rumored decrease in state aid takes place. They plan to hold a series of open meetings to get public feedback before making any decision. They have asked you to serve on the building committee and to prepare a recommendation that reflects your own and your faculty's opinions.

Case Questions

1. What is your immediate reaction to each of the four plans?
2. How do you go about formulating the recommendation requested?
3. What are your personal and professional considerations in this matter?
4. What role do you think you should play as a member of the building committee?
5. Would you be comfortable endorsing one of the plans? Would you endorse one of the plans with stipulations or modifications? Would you want to suggest another alternative?
6. What role should the faculty play in making this decision?
7. What role do you see for yourself in selling the proposal to the taxpayers?

SUGGESTED ACTIVITY: Describe in a $1\frac{1}{2}$- to 2-page paper how you would acquire the background necessary to make informed decisions on physical plant concerns.

PROBLEM 8—SAMANTHA: A CONFLICT OF VALUES

Samantha is a student in Sandra Johnson's third-grade class. She is a tall, wiry girl who presents a very tough facade. She has often been disruptive in class and typically insists on being the first to have or do everything. Ms. Johnson has tried hard to get Samantha to share and cooperate, but Samantha refuses to do so. She has alienated most of her classmates.

Today Samantha pushed into line in the cafeteria by shoving Larry Saunders out of his place. Larry objected and Samantha said that if he couldn't hold his spot at the front of the line, he didn't deserve it. She then asked what he was going to do about it and raised her fists as if to fight. Larry went to Ms. Johnson and told her what Samantha had done. Ms. Johnson went to Samantha and told her to go to the end of the line and stop intimidating other students. Samantha refused. Ms. Johnson pulled her out of line and brought her to your office.

Ms. Johnson is visibly upset and, in front of Samantha, tells you that she has had it with the girl and her pushy mother. She now wants you to deal with it. Ms. Johnson says that she will not have Samantha riding roughshod over everyone else. All the talk in the world has not helped. She wants you to do something.

You phone Samantha's mother, Ms. Hardy, and ask her to come in. About a half hour later she arrives. She does not greet you in any way but, rather, demands to know what was so urgent that she had to leave work to come in. You tell her what happened. She says that she is proud of the way Samantha behaved. Ms. Hardy says that she was pushed around all her life and that she has taught Samantha to stick up for herself and not take guff from anyone, especially boys.

You say that Samantha was clearly the antagonist in this situation. Larry had done nothing to deserve being shoved out of line. You point out that there is a big difference between standing up for yourself and being aggressive and disruptive. She responds that you would never have called a boy's mother in for such a petty offense but that because it was a girl you made a big deal out of it. You respond that you called her in because this incident was only one of many and that you and the school have a responsibility to see that all children treat others fairly.

Ms. Hardy goes on to say that she wants this matter closed, that Samantha has been humiliated enough by being dragged to the office, and that she will not permit you to punish or persecute her daughter. It is a tough world, and she is raising her daughter to be tough in order to cope with it. She suggests that you spend your time on more worthwhile things and keep your nose out of how she raises her daughter.

Case Questions

1. How do you handle the situation from here?
2. What rule of thumb do you use to decide when to call a parent out of work or when to call a parent into your office at all?
3. If you see that a parent is hostile or is becoming hostile, what are some strategies you can use to defuse the situation?

4. When there is a direct conflict between traditional modes of behavior and values and the behavior and values espoused by a parent, what do you do?

5. After this immediate problem is resolved, what strategies will you suggest to Ms. Johnson to deal with Samantha in the future?

SUGGESTED ACTIVITY: Find out what the research indicates about the causes of overaggressive behavior in children.

PROBLEM 9—THE TEACHERS'-ROOM RUMOR MILL: DEALING WITH DAMAGED REPUTATIONS

Part 1—The Rumor Is Started

In briefing you after you were hired but before your first day on the job, your superintendent told you that it would be best if you avoided the faculty room in your school. You were told that although the faculty was professional and competent in many ways, it really became nasty and factionalized in the teachers' lounge, especially at lunchtime. The superintendent suggested that you let the faculty have that room as its own space and as an arena for faculty members to vent their spleens.

You have noticed that several teachers choose to eat their lunches in their classrooms and that the three male teachers sit together in one corner of the cafeteria to eat. You have generally been too busy to bother taking any regular lunch, but when you do eat, it is usually either in your office or in the cafeteria with the students. You generally ignore what goes on in the teacher's room.

Today the president of the Parent-Teacher Organization (PTO) has come in to say that she has heard that Andy Valentine, the music teacher, is gay. She says she has nothing against gays, but if what she has heard is true, she wants to make sure that he isn't providing a negative model to the students. You ask her where she heard the rumor. She says that one of the teachers, whom she will not name, told her and said that Mr. Valentine had been seen coming out of a gay bar in a nearby city.

You respond that you have no reason to feel that Mr. Valentine is providing a negative model to the students in any way and that he has done nothing to call attention to his private life. The president replies that she does not want to spread rumors, cause anyone to lose his or her job, or accuse anyone of anything improper. You press her to find out which faculty member told her about Mr. Valentine. She refuses to say, but she suggests that perhaps you should investigate what is going on. Then she excuses herself and leaves.

Case Questions

1. What problems do you see here?
2. What is your next move?

3. What are the legal and ethical issues involved?

4. If you elect to investigate the matter, what do you hope to discover, and how will you conduct your investigation? If you choose not to investigate, explain your reasons?

5. What, if anything, do you say to Andy Valentine at this juncture?

Part 2—Damage Control

You have decided to investigate how the rumor about Andy Valentine started and spread. It soon becomes obvious that it originated with the teachers who use the faculty lounge during the second lunch. From one of the teachers who has second lunch free but chooses to eat in her room, you hear that the reason she avoids the faculty room at lunchtime is that the clique in there during that time has always been vicious and gossips constantly. She says they have torn apart almost everyone in the district at one time or another. She advises you not to listen to anything they say and tells you that if they did see Andy in that part of the city, it was because they went as a group to a bar in that neighborhood to see male strippers two Saturdays ago. She suggests that if people want to point a finger at Andy, you should have them explain what brought them into proximity with that gay bar and how they knew what it was in the first place. She says that she supports Andy fully and that, to the best of her knowledge, he has always acted professionally. She concludes by saying that what happens in people's private lives is no one else's business.

Case Questions

1. With this information in hand, what do you do?

2. What does this information do to your estimation of the second-lunch clique, the teachers who avoid the faculty room at lunchtime, the president of the PTO, and Andy Valentine?

3. What additional information do you need, if any, to determine how to proceed?

SUGGESTED ACTIVITY: Find out under what circumstances the district may become legally responsible if Andy Valentine's career is hurt by the accusations concerning his sexual preference.

PROBLEM 10—PRIORITIZING: HOW TO MANAGE A FULL DAY'S PROBLEMS IN A HALF HOUR

You have been at a budget meeting in the central office with the other administrators in the district. You get back to your building at 2:58, two minutes before the dismissal bell. Your secretary is on the phone but hands you the following messages:

1. The boys' locker room has been flooded because someone stuffed paper towels into all of the toilets and kept flushing. The custodian has been working to pull out all the towels, but it is going slowly, and the locker room is still flooded. You know that the junior high boys will be here for basketball practice very soon.
2. Mrs. Schmidt called, wanting to see you this afternoon about her son Philip. She said it was urgent but would not say what the problem was. She will speak only to you.
3. Karen Hold, a second-grade teacher, asked permission to leave immediately after student dismissal in order to make a dentist appointment.
4. Two sixth-grade girls will be coming to see you as soon as they are dismissed, to get your permission to hold an after-school dance in the cafeteria next Friday for sixth-graders only.
5. Dr. Sousa from State University called about placing a student teacher in your school next semester. She would like you to call her back before 4:00. Her number is 584-8866.
6. An elementary principal from a neighboring district called to get a recommendation about Nancy Rivers, who used to be an aide in your building. She is now applying for a teaching position in Mapleton School. Your colleague would like a response before 4:00. The phone number is 674-6215.
7. Eight letters that should go out today are on your desk, awaiting your signature.
8. Two fourth-graders, Frank Russo and Derrick Foster, are waiting outside your office. They were fighting on the playground after lunch and have been sitting there since then. Mrs. Obanski sent them down.

Case Questions

1. How do you prioritize these demands for your attention?
2. How and in what order do you take care of each of them?
3. Should someone have brought any of these matters to your attention by calling you at the superintendent's office and interrupting the meeting?

SUGGESTED ACTIVITY: Go back through the situations presented in this case, and write down how you would have responded to them if you had been in your office all day. Compare those responses with the likely outcomes of the same circumstances when presented to you all at once at the end of the school day.

PROBLEM 11—THE BREAKFAST PROGRAM: STATE VERSUS SCHOOL BOARD

For longer than anyone currently on the school board has served, the state has encouraged districts to offer a free breakfast to students who are eligible for a free hot lunch. The board has consistently voted not to offer such a program. The grounds for declining to offer the program have been as follows:

1. Although the food would be provided by the federal government, the cost of preparing and serving the food and supervising the students would have to be picked up by the district.
2. Virtually all the families that would be eligible for free breakfast are on welfare, and part of their welfare grant and food stamp allowance is for serving their children breakfast. By offering free breakfast, the schools would be providing government food to those who had already been given government food for the same meal.
3. The schools are already being forced to take on the role of parents; the program would encourage parents to relinquish even more responsibility.
4. Many of the children of school board members refuse to eat breakfast, despite their parents' efforts, and they do okay in school.
5. The free breakfast program would have to be offered in the cafeteria, and that is the area where children are allowed to stay in bad weather if they arrive too early to enter the classroom wing of the building.
6. Many free-lunch recipients provide false information in order to claim eligibility. The board once tried to eliminate the false claims, but the legal hassle was so great that they gave up trying to enforce the standards. Now they give free or reduced-price lunch to anyone who claims to be eligible. The addition of free breakfast would just add insult to injury.
7. The program would be just one more nonacademic problem that would take the focus of the school away from education and would create more paperwork and bureaucracy.
8. Many of the eligible students stay up far too late as it is. A free breakfast program would force them to get up earlier, making them even more tired and therefore less able to learn.
9. If a free-breakfast program were offered, the bus runs for all students might have to begin earlier. If they did, more students would be on school grounds for an extended period. That extended period would provide additional opportunity for before-school problems and would place extra supervision demands on the staff.

This year the state began requiring all schools with more than 50 students eligible for free hot lunch to offer free breakfast. The regulation would force the district to begin the program it had resisted so consistently. The members of the school board were furious. They considered the regulation another state infringement on local autonomy. In a split vote, the board voted not to comply with the new requirement. The superintendent said she could sympathize with the board's feelings on the matter, but she advised them to reconsider their decision because it could put state aid in jeopardy. The board reconsidered the measure, but the final vote was the same.

The local newspaper ran the board's decision as its lead story. The next day the commissioner phoned the superintendent to inform her that, if the board did not reverse its decision, state aid would be withheld and the members of the board, including those who had voted for the program, would face arrest. A heated debate spread throughout the community, but in the end the board agreed under protest to provide free breakfast. Everyone thought the crisis was past.

The board has ordered the cafeteria workers to prepare bags, each with a single-serving box of cereal, a small carton of milk, and a small carton of orange juice. Students eligible for free lunch may go through the cafeteria on their way home and pick up a bag if they wish. The students are to be told to eat the food before they leave for school in the morning. Very few students take advantage of the offer.

Case Questions

1. What is your assessment of the board's arguments against providing free breakfast?
2. What unstated reasons might the board have for refusing to provide free breakfast?
3. Is the free-breakfast program a good idea? Why or why not?
4. Would the state have had grounds for arresting the board members for failure to provide free breakfast if the board had refused to alter its original position? Would there have been grounds for arresting the board members who voted to provide the program? If so, what are those grounds? Does the board's new position put it in compliance with state regulations?
5. Could the superintendent have acted differently? If so, what should she have done?
6. What do you think of the way the board chose to comply with the regulation? Do you think the state will be satisfied with that solution?
7. What do you think will happen next?

SUGGESTED ACTIVITY: Write a letter to the president of the school board, outlining the reasons the board should reconsider its refusal to offer a free-breakfast program or the reasons it should stick to its original decision.

PROBLEM 12—PARENTS MAKE A CHOICE: SELECTING A CURRICULUM

Three years ago the school board decided that all elementary teachers were to adopt a new social studies program called *You and the Whole World Around You*. The program had been constructed to be politically correct. It dealt with values clarification, multicultural issues, decision making, stress reduction, self-assessment, self-motivation, interpersonal relationship skills, human rights, racism, sexism, ecological issues, and other current social issues. The program incorporated very little history except to describe the suppression of one group by another. The idea was that history, government, and geography could best be learned in Grades 7–12. *You and the Whole World Around You*, usually called simply *Whole World*, was intended to develop the student's sense of self worth, tolerance, and social justice. It addressed the affective domain far more than the cognitive.

When it was introduced, there was bitter dissent from the teachers and several parents. Some teachers had been using a good deal of the *Whole World* material already; others strongly resisted change. Some teachers began applying to other districts so that they would not have to use the approach. Others protested that the program was devoid of real content, defied systematic instruction, did not cover the material prescribed by the state standards, did not prepare students for standardized tests, forced secular humanism down the students' throats, and did not give students a foundation in such skill areas as graph and map reading, research, and drawing conclusions from collected research material. The former principal, Mrs. Mumford, has told you that she did everything she could think of to encourage the teachers to adhere to the board's decision with open minds and a spirit of cooperation. Some teachers filed grievances to challenge the forced change. All the grievances were denied, but the board did say that teachers could include instruction in the skill areas they had delineated.

All the teachers were given new materials and training to enable them to implement the program. Except for one veteran teacher who had been in your school well over 40 years and who is a venerated institution in town, all the teachers eventually complied. That teacher continued to teach geography and government to her class. No one on the board or in the administration was willing to challenge her directly, and everyone expected her to retire soon. Her students had always done better on standardized tests than students in other classes, and that tradition continued after the introduction of *Whole World*.

The school board hired Jeff Klisch to fill the newly created position of curriculum coordinator last year, at the same meeting where it hired you. Although Jeff has K–12 responsibilities, one of the primary reasons given for creating the new position was that your school had grown to the point where it needed more than one full-time administrator. Your predecessor had argued that a half-time assistant principal would be a better choice than a K–12 curriculum coordinator who had no line authority and who would report directly to the superintendent. The decision to hire a curriculum coordinator was one of the reasons Mrs. Mumford gave for taking early retirement. In her view, she had lost the confidence of the board when they rejected her proposal of a half-time assistant principal and hired Jeff.

You have found Jeff to be an asset and have become comfortable working with him. His schedule is to spend most of his time during school hours either at the high school or in the central office. He is in your building primarily after school, working in curriculum committees with the faculty. The superintendent advised you, shortly after you began, to stay as clear of the *Whole World* controversy as possible, and to this point you have.

Jeff, on the other hand, has been involved with *Whole World* since his first day as coordinator. The school year had barely begun when he realized the morass the elementary social studies program had become. No one had trained the two teachers new to the school this year in the program, and they struggled through the material as best they could. Some teachers had become devotees of the program, and others had drifted slowly but steadily back to the traditional program. Most were teaching a muddled mixture of *Whole World* and the traditional program.

Jeff had no difficulty finding people who were willing to describe in great detail the process by which *Whole World* had been introduced into the system. It was obvious that it took very little to rekindle the old debate. Two members of the school board who had strongly supported *Whole World* had recently lost their reelection bids, and the present board was much less committed to the program. Jeff's questions made it clear that there were three easily identifiable camps: the traditionalists, the *Whole World* advocates, and those who wanted to retain some elements of both programs. That split in opinion reflected the thinking not only of the teachers, but also of the PTO. The controversy, which had lain dormant for the past two years, took on new life.

Whole World was a program with which Jeff had been only superficially acquainted. He had seen many innovations, most of them revisions of older programs, come and go. It had been his experience that some students did well with virtually any program, others did poorly with all approaches, and some did better with one method than another. He believed that most techniques worked well with some segment of the population and that there was no method that was best for everyone all the time. He had seen good programs discarded because they had become unfashionable. When a new method was adopted, it seemed to Jeff, no one analyzed the existing system to determine what its strengths and weaknesses were and what sort of student did well under that approach. People seemed to forget that when they embraced something new, they rejected something they had been doing. The loss was seldom discovered quickly and in some cases was never realized until the old method was upgraded and became the new approach in a never-ending cycle.

Jeff's first task was to become familiar with the *Whole World* program. He began with the training tapes and manuals the district had purchased when the program was first introduced. He spoke with the faculty, both those who reported using the program and those who had partially or largely abandoned it. He formed a committee by selecting three natural leaders among the faculty, teachers who were well respected by their colleagues and by parents.

The first step taken by the committee was for each member to delineate the strengths of each approach and describe in a detailed curriculum map social studies instruction in the grade she or he taught. That part of the assignment required considerable work, but it was not as difficult as what was to follow. The next step was to identify students who seemed to do well under each of the approaches. The teachers' instructions were to concentrate, not on those students who did well across the board, but rather on those who seemed to do better with one of the three particular social studies approaches than they did generally. They also looked at those students who seemed to do less well in social studies than they did in other subjects.

When developing the detailed curriculum maps, all three teachers found that they were automatically making revisions although they had intended simply to record accurately what they had been doing. All three were surprised when they realized what had happened. Once they began grappling with the question which type of student did best under which approach, one of them remarked that at least the development of the curriculum map had produced some valuable outcomes.

The best they could do with the analysis of student success under each approach was muddled. A few characteristics did emerge, but most of them came from thinking about those students who did not do well rather than from the more successful cases. The teachers found themselves wondering about each student's parents' religious beliefs, social status, and other characteristics when trying to discern differences in the effectiveness of the three approaches.

When the group was satisfied that it had accomplished all it could, Jeff approached the superintendent and the board about allowing him to use an upcoming in-service day to work with the elementary staff on the social studies question. When it was pointed out that such use of the in-service day would not create any additional expenditures, the board agreed.

On the in-service day, the three teachers on the committee described in detail what they had found about the approaches they used and distributed copies of the curriculum maps they had developed. Each teacher on the faculty was asked to select from the three approaches the one he or she liked best. Approximately one third of the faculty selected the strict *Whole World* program, one third the traditional program, and the remainder the mixed approach. Since the division was not quite even, a few teachers without strong opinions on the matter were asked to volunteer to shift approaches so that there would be a balance. The faculty noted that the kindergarten and first-grade programs were minimally affected by *Whole World* and that those grades provided a neutral assignment for teachers.

The faculty was divided into three groups according to choice of approach. Each group was given the task of developing curriculum guides for every grade except the one for which a curriculum map had already been completed by the committee member who exemplified that group's approach. The *Whole World* group and the traditionalists completed their assignment by the end of the day. The mixed-approach group needed two additional one-hour sessions to finish.

Jeff convinced the board and the superintendent that the next step was to make the grade assignments for the following year in such a way as to ensure that each of the three approaches would have one advocate at each grade level. It was further decided that students at all grade levels in the school would change teachers for social studies and that social studies would be taught at the same time among the teachers at each grade level.

The next step was to develop a one-page summary of each of the three approaches. Parents would be asked to review the summaries and select the approach they preferred for their children. Those who had no opinion could leave the choice to their child's present teacher. Parents would also be asked to indicate how important the matter was to them. There would be an open house so that interested parents could find out more about the programs and speak directly to the teachers.

The information sheets were sent home with the students, there was an article in the local paper, and an announcement about the open house was mailed home. Jeff had decided not to try to force the parents into making a decision. He thought there was enough information available to afford those parents who cared ample opportunity to choose. Once the parents who responded had their children placed in the program of their choice, the faculty could balance the classes with children whose parents had not responded, had shown no preference, or had asked the teachers to make the choice.

Among the parents who responded, the traditional approach proved the most popular, and virtually all slots in those classes were filled. A few faculty members objected to being reassigned to a different grade level, and those objections were considered on an individual basis. The board and the superintendent were surprised that the selection process had gone so smoothly. The program is all set to go into operation next year. At the end of March of next year, the choice system will be evaluated and a decision reached on its future.

Case Questions

1. Could this choice system have been put into place if the school board had not changed? Why or why not?
2. What is your opinion of the way Jeff went about instituting the choice system?
3. Do you agree with Jeff's assumptions? Why or why not?
4. Do you feel parents should have been required to decide? Why or why not?
5. Do you feel the system will succeed? Why or why not?
6. So far the choice system has been confined to one subject. Could it be extended to more than one subject, or would that make scheduling logistically impossible?
7. What types of choices should parents be permitted to make?
8. What problems do you think the choice system that has been implemented might create?
9. Should parents be given the opportunity to make curriculum choices at all?
10. Examine and describe the process Jeff went through with regard to the *Whole World* program. Why did he approach the problem in that way? Do you think there was a better or more efficient way? If so, how would you have approached the problem?
11. What do you think of the superintendent's advice to stay out of the *Whole World* controversy? What should your role be in such a situation?
12. What were the superintendent's probable motives or intentions in offering you that advice?
13. What process would you follow to implement a new curriculum?

SUGGESTED ACTIVITIES: (a) In 500 words or less, write a description of the appropriate goals and objectives of an elementary social studies program. (b) Go through the major events in this case, beginning with the introduction of *Whole World.* Assume that the curriculum was first discussed by the school board on September 15. Assign an appropriate month, day, and year to each development in the case. Once that time line is complete, state briefly the actions you would have taken had you been hired as the new curriculum coordinator instead of Jeff. Put those actions in their correct positions on the time line. If you believe your actions would have altered the sequence of events, describe how.

PROBLEM 13—FACULTY MEMBERS COME TO YOU FOR ADVICE: SEEING PROBLEMS THROUGH THE EYES OF A TEACHER AGAIN

Note: Except when otherwise stated, for the following short scenarios, assume you are in your office after school when the teachers come to you for advice.

A. A kindergarten teacher, Paula Ableson, comes to you obviously distressed. There is a very vocal parents' group in the district where you teach. The group feels very strongly that children with AIDS should not be allowed in school, at least not in the lower grades, where by the nature of their activities there is frequent physical contact and some chance for the exchange of bodily fluids. At the beginning of the academic year, the nurse indicated to Ms. Ableson that one of the children in her room has AIDS. At a PTO meeting, some members of the parents' group confronted Ms. Ableson and said they knew that a child in her room has AIDS. They asked her straight out if Michael Brooks has AIDS, claiming that they have a right to know and that she is obliged to tell them. They said that the protection of their children vastly outweighed his right to privacy. Michael Brooks is not the child the nurse informed Ms. Ableson about. Ms. Ableson told the parents that she had no reason to believe that their children had any reason to fear contact with Michael. She refused to say anything else, citing confidentiality. The parents were not satisfied and said that she would be hearing more from them about this matter. She says the confrontation was so unpleasant that she feels a threat hanging over her head and doesn't know what to expect or do.

Case Questions

1. How do you respond?
2. Did Ms. Ableson act appropriately?
3. How can you defuse the situation?
4. Did the nurse act properly?
5. What are the policies in your state and district about the release of medical information? Do you really know, or are you making assumptions?

B. Fifth-grade teacher Marina Pulaski comes to you. She has a student named Karen in her room. Karen's fourth-grade teacher, Ruth Obanski, has come into Mrs. Pulaski's room several days in a row to warn her about Karen. Mrs. Obanski says Karen is sneaky and is a cheat and a liar. She claims that she wanted to retain her but you ordered that she be promoted to fifth grade. Mrs. Obanski persists in asking what Karen has been up to lately. Mrs. Pulaski reports that she has given her colleague noncommital, polite replies but that she keeps coming back. So far Mrs. Pulaski has not noticed anything special about Karen, but the school year is less than two weeks old. Mrs. Pulaski now wants to know whether she should be concerned about Karen, how she should deal with Mrs. Obanski, and what really happened last year.

Mrs. Obanski and Karen were a real problem for you last spring. Karen had been caught stealing from other students on two occasions and had been caught in a few lies. There had been a parent conference, and as far as you knew, Karen had stopped stealing. Mrs. Obanski, however, continued to accuse the girl every time anything negative happened and there was no obvious culprit. You dealt with the teacher several times regarding her accusations against Karen. Now that the girl was in fifth grade, you thought the problem would be over.

Case Questions

1. What do you tell Mrs. Pulaski?
2. How do you deal with Mrs. Obanski?
3. How can you prevent teachers from persecuting students?

C. Sharon Massi teaches fourth grade. She buzzes the office on the intercom asking that you come to her room as soon as possible. When you arrive, her class is at recess. She meets you in the hall in front of the closed door to her room. She says that Kevin is inside. He is a tough kid, bright enough, but constantly in trouble. Two parents who had obviously been in contact with each other called Ms. Massi at home last night and complained that Kevin has tried to touch their daughters on their breasts and has whispered sexually inappropriate things to them. The parents said that if something wasn't done the next day, they would take matters into their own hands.

Ms. Massi kept Kevin in at recess and confronted him about the complaints. At first he denied everything, but she acted on instinct and pressed the investigation further by asking what happens at home. Kevin started to cry and get angry. He said his mother touches his groin area all the time, and if it's all right for her, he can do it, too. Ms. Massi says the fact that Kevin waits until there is no one around before he touches the girls indicates that he knows it is not right, just as it is not right for anyone to touch his groin. Her class will be returning very shortly.

Case Questions

1. What do you think of the way Ms. Massi has handled the situation up to this point?
2. What is the policy in your district regarding the reporting of child abuse? What is the law on that matter?
3. What training should you provide for your staff with regard to recognizing and reporting abuse?
4. What will you do now?

D.   Laura Eldridge, one of your first-grade teachers, comes to you to say that she is concerned about Martha Feinstein, one of her grade-level colleagues, who is known to be especially kind and generous. Mrs. Feinstein has taken pity on a poor little girl named Tanya. Tanya's mother has three children younger than Tanya, and her husband has left her. The mother is on welfare, and rumors are that she has a steady stream of men coming to the house. The police have been called several times by the neighbors because of loud parties and fights in the apartment. Tanya comes to school without breakfast and in filthy, shabby clothes. She is often tardy or absent. Mrs. Feinstein has taken Tanya on outings and brought her toys. Almost every day the teacher gives Tanya food. In fact she now brings extra food, anticipating that Tanya will need it.

The end of the school year is a week away. Mrs. Feinstein has told Laura Eldridge she intends to ask Tanya's mother if Tanya can spend the summer with her. Mrs. Feinstein wants to know what her colleague thinks of the idea. Ms. Eldridge has serious misgivings about the idea and has come to you for advice on how to respond to her friend.

Case Questions

1. What are the boundaries of the teacher-student relationship?
2. Are they different for younger children than for older ones?
3. What happens to that relationship when the student is no longer in the teacher's class?
4. What are the legal issues here?
5. What do you advise Ms. Eldridge to tell her colleague?
6. Do you become directly involved at this point? If so, how?
7. Does what Ms. Eldridge describes about Tanya constitute neglect? If so, what are you obliged to do about it?

E.   The school board recently determined that the district will use the *Whole Language* approach in Grades K–6. The primary-grade teachers have used the method for several years, but the upper-grade teachers have not. The decision was made unexpectedly. You protested that *Whole Language* could not be implemented without preparation. The board allowed you a half-day in-service to prepare the staff and instructed you to work with the curriculum coordinator to phase in the program as quickly as possible. You checked with the curriculum coordinator and found that the *Whole Language* decision was as much a surprise to him as it was to you.

Diane Taylor, one of your sixth-grade teachers, has come to you, saying that she feels ill prepared to implement the program. She is willing to try, and she believes the concept can work at the upper elementary level, but she relates that many of her colleagues say privately that the board of education was sold a bill of goods. They feel that *Whole Language* is OK for the primary grades but inappropriate for the upper grades. Some of the teachers are saying that they will pay the program lip service, but nothing more. Those teachers say that you have been put in the middle and have no choice but to go along with the board's decision, but that you don't like the decision and will not really try to enforce it.

Case Questions

1. How do you respond to Ms. Taylor?
2. What do you think of the board decision? Might you have responded in a more proactive way? If so, how?
3. How seriously do you take the information which has just been presented to you?
4. Do you need to investigate further? If so, how would you go about doing it?
5. If Ms. Taylor is reporting the reaction of the other upper-elementary teachers accurately, what does it say about their relationship with you? What, if anything, will you do about it?
6. How, in general, do you proceed from this point onward?
7. What role should the curriculum coordinator play?
8. Think back to Problem 12. The board's decision on the *Whole World* program has been altered, and your entire staff has undergone a process of introspection. Just as that controversy is settled, the board makes another sweeping curriculum decision without warning. Does this suggest that the district's administrators need to review their relationship to the board? If so, what might be done? Specifically, what role should you and the curriculum coordinator take with regard to this and future curriculum decisions?
9. What might the superintendent have done when the board announced its decision to implement *Whole Language* so abruptly?

F. Maria Lopez, one of your third-grade teachers, has come to see you. She takes some time to come around to her primary objective, but eventually she says that she is concerned about Rebecca, the student teacher in Miss Kennedy's room. You are aware that Ms. Lopez and Miss Kennedy have a strained relationship. She reports that Rebecca simply observed for the first two days and that on the third day Miss Kennedy handed over her seating chart, lesson plans, and grade book and said the class was Rebecca's. Miss Kennedy then reportedly spent virtually the entire day in the faculty lounge.

When Ms. Lopez asked Miss Kennedy why she had left her student teacher alone so abruptly instead of easing her into the position and offering support, Miss Kennedy said that the only way to learn to teach was by teaching. If anything drastic happened, Miss Kennedy said, she would be ready to step in. Besides, if she were to stay in the room, the students would look to her for the answers and not transfer their attention to the student teacher. Miss Kennedy said that she intended to start observing once the students had completed the transfer.

Ms. Lopez reports that Rebecca has started coming to her for advice and feedback. Rebecca supposedly called Miss Kennedy a jerk and said that she had contacted her university supervisor to request a change of placement. Ms. Lopez claims that Miss Kennedy has even left the building for extended periods during the last few days. Ms. Lopez says that Miss Kennedy is being paid for her services as a cooperating teacher and has clearly not been doing her job. Ms. Lopez wants you to intervene on behalf of the student teacher.

Case Questions

1. There are three possibilities here: Ms. Lopez's observations may be accurate, and Miss Kennedy may really be neglecting her student teacher. Miss Kennedy may be reacting responsibly, and Ms. Lopez may be misreporting or misinterpreting the situation. Or the truth may lie somewhere in the middle. How do you investigate the matter?

2. Consider each of the three possibilities in turn, and decide how you would handle the situation in each instance.

3. What should your role be with student teachers? With the university? With the cooperating teachers?

4. What professional responsibilities do you have for training new teachers? Training people to become teachers?

G. Steve Roth, fifth-grade teacher, has come to see you. He says that he has been working for three weeks on adding fractions with unlike denominators. The students seemed to be learning the material, but last Friday he gave the class a test, and nearly half the students failed. Eight students said that $\frac{1}{4} + \frac{1}{3} = \frac{2}{7}$. He cannot imagine why the results were so poor. The fourth-grade teachers were supposed to have introduced the idea of the lowest common denominator, and he spent more time this year than last on this type of problem, but many students obviously have not learned it. He had intended to go on to changing fractions to decimals, but now he is unsure what he should do. Four students had perfect scores on the test, and three others also earned A's. There were only four B's, two C's, three D's, and twelve F's. Some of his better students did poorly. He cannot account for the odd distribution of grades. He is unsure what to do about the students who mastered the material, what to do about those who did poorly, or how much more time he can spend on the addition of fractions. He is afraid he will not complete the curriculum for the year.

Case Questions

1. What possibilities do you consider when reviewing the test results?
2. Do you find the test results surprising?
3. What additional information might be useful in determining the cause of the strange grade distribution?
4. What will you advise Mr. Roth to do?

SUGGESTED ACTIVITY: List the types of concerns teachers should bring to their principal. If you feel new teachers should have greater access than veteran teachers, indicate the extent to which that should be true.

CHAPTER SUMMARY

The problems in this chapter were designed to allow you to gain insight into your personal values and administrative style as well as to expose you to situations typically faced by elementary school administrators.

The first area you should explore is your basic motivation. In the 1970s it was popular to group all motivation into three categories: power, affiliation, and goal attainment. The term *power* is self-explanatory. Affiliation, in this context, means positive interaction with other people, liking them and being liked. Goal attainment is the accomplishment of something beyond what presently exists. In this view of motivation, no one is driven exclusively by only one of the three forces, and each of us shifts from one primary motivator to another in certain circumstances. There remains, however, a pattern we can recognize. Once we recognize that pattern within ourselves, we are in a better position to understand how we make decisions. People who are power oriented will find solutions to the problems presented in this chapter that are significantly different from those found by people motivated primarily by affiliation or goal attainment.

Each of us also has secondary and tertiary motivators. The degree to which we fit into each of the categories also makes a difference. If you are 50% power oriented, 30% goal oriented, and 20% affiliation oriented, you respond differently from someone who is 85% power motivated, 10% goal oriented, and 5% affiliation oriented, even though you have the same primary, secondary, and tertiary motivators as the other person.

Our ability to work with others is affected by both our estimation of their motivators and their estimation of ours. Two very power-oriented people may have difficulty working together. Two affiliation-motivated people may work well together but not accomplish much. The combinations are nearly endless when you consider primary, secondary, and tertiary motivators and the degrees of each. By recognizing your own orientation within this paradigm and the orientation of those around you, you can sometimes alter your approach to arrive at better resolutions. Understanding the motivations of others is especially important when you select people to serve on committees, share duties, or share space and resources.

Using the framework just described, examine the decisions you have made about the problems presented in this chapter. See if your motivational orientation shows and if what comes through is what you imagined it would be. Review the research on the motivation of administrators, and determine where you fit within each theory.

The second area you should explore is the degree to which you act autocratically or democratically. Despotic administrators often alienate subordinates, fail to use the expertise of others, and must maintain constant pressure to enforce their decisions. Democratic leaders who rely extensively on shared decision making are sometimes seen as indecisive, inefficient, and weak. Very few administrators, if any, can survive long if they adhere unalterably to either end of the continuum.

In the middle are those of us who delegate, seek input, and consult. We continually move up and down the continuum as we are faced with different situations. It is important, however, to recognize that most of us have a zone within the continuum from which we usually function and to which we usually return. It may change over time, but once we reach maturity, our comfort zone becomes relatively stable. We are capable of consciously moving to another point on the continuum, but it takes great effort and repeated success at that new point for us to firmly establish a new position.

Use the problems in this chapter to explore how you move up and down the continuum and where your comfort zone is. There are other models of administration that are not located on this continuum. For now, however, consider the autocrat-democrat dichotomy presented here.

The third area you should examine is your attitudes toward the people described. How do you feel about pushy parents, school bullies, timid teachers, gossips, homosexual teachers, victims, natural leaders among the faculty, and so on? Which are most difficult for you to deal with? How do you adjust your own behaviors when encountering each of those different types?

The fourth area you should review at this juncture is how you know when you have enough information to make a sound decision about a particular matter. There is always more that you can find out, but at some point what is still unknown is not going to influence the action you take. Part of your decision will be based on the significance of the problem to you and the amount of time and effort you determine it deserves. In the cases presented here, you have no options. The material you have to work with is given, and no more is available unless you choose to generate it. You may, however, decide that some of what is presented is not germane and should not affect your actions.

It is also quite probable that you would have departed from the course described before the events unfolded as they did. If so, describe first what you would have done differently, and then assume that you had taken the action depicted in the narrative, and proceed from there.

In subsequent chapters of this book, we will examine different issues that may help you evolve as a professional. Periodically review your decisions in past cases in light of the motivations, administrative style, decision-making techniques, and attitudes you have developed and explored.

There are a great many theoretical approaches to administration and variations of those approaches. The activities suggested in this summary focus on only a few possibilities. Your instructor may direct you to respond to the cases described in any number of ways, which may or may not include the ones suggested in this summary.

There were two reasons for describing the setting for the cases in this chapter in detail. The first was to encourage and enable you to assume the role of an elementary principal more fully. The second was to help you begin to assess the extent to which the nature of the setting will influence your decision-making process and the decisions themselves. As you move on to other chapters, the role of the setting will be explored again.

As a final activity to complete before moving on to the next chapter, consider the characteristics that make an elementary school different from schools at other levels. Informal traditional wisdom would include the following:

1. Elementary parents are much more likely to be involved in the school and its programs than secondary parents.
2. Elementary students, especially in the primary grades, present a far different set of characteristics and problems than secondary students and must be treated differently.
3. Elementary staffs are almost always overwhelmingly female and much more child oriented and more receptive to cooperative efforts and change than are secondary staffs.
4. Before- and after-school child care is a much greater problem for elementary parents than for secondary parents.
5. Elementary principals and staffs have far fewer after-school and evening activities than secondary educators have.
6. Issues concerning child abuse and custody are far more likely to arise in elementary schools than in secondary schools.

There are, of course, a great many more traditional characteristics that could be listed.

Review the six assumptions listed and any others you are able to generate. Determine the extent to which they are true and the extent to which they are changing. Then list the characteristics you believe distinguish an elementary school now, and speculate about where elementary education is heading in the 21st century.

SUMMARY QUESTIONS

1. Which of the situations described in this chapter seems most likely to lead to more serious problems in the future?

2. Which situations did you find the most difficult to deal with? Why?

3. Which situations, if any, do you feel you should have reported to the central office? What is the basis for your response?

4. Now that you have grappled with all the situations, are there any that you might now choose to respond to differently?

5. What was your basis for making the decisions you made about each situation?

6. If you really had been hired as the principal, what steps would you have taken to prepare yourself for your new position? What would you have wanted to know about the recent history of the school? The district? The community? What steps would you have taken to gather that information?

SUGGESTED READING

Alexander, K., & Alexander, M. D. (1984). *The law of schools, students, and teachers in a nutshell.* St. Paul, MN: West.

Allen, D. W. (1992). *Schools for a new century: A conservative approach to radical school reform.* Westport, CT: Praeger.

Anderson, B. F. (1980). *The complete thinker: A handbook of techniques for creative and critical problem solving.* Englewood Cliffs, NJ: Prentice-Hall.

Arnold, J. D. (1992). *The complete problem solver: A total system for competitive decision making.* New York: Wiley.

Black, J., & English, F. (1986). *What they don't tell you in schools of education about school administration.* Lancaster, PA: Technomic.

Blumberg, A., & Greenfield, W. (1980). *The effective principal: Perspectives on school leadership.* Boston, MA: Allyn & Bacon.

Carew, J. V., & Lightfoot, S. L. (1979). *Beyond bias: Perspectives on classrooms.* Cambridge, MA: Harvard University Press.

Cruickshank, D. R. (1980). *Teaching is tough.* Englewood Cliffs, NJ: Prentice-Hall.

Drake, T., & Roe, W. (1986). *The principalship.* New York: Macmillan.

Glickman, Carl D. (1989). *Supervision of instruction: A developmental approach* (2nd ed.). Boston, MA: Allyn & Bacon.

Hanson, E. (1985). *Educational administration and organizational behavior* (2nd ed.). Boston, MA: Allyn & Bacon.

Hess, A. G. (Ed.). (1992). *Empowering teachers and parents: School restructuring through the eyes of anthropologists.* Westport, CT: Bergin & Garvey.

Hoy, W., & Forsyth, P. (1986). *Effective supervision: Theory into practice.* New York: Random House.

Kepner, C. H., & Tregoe, B. B. (1965). *The rational manager: A systematic approach to problem solving and decision making.* New York: McGraw-Hill.

Levine, M. (1988). *Effective problem solving.* Englewood Cliffs, NJ: Prentice-Hall.

Lieberman, A. (Ed.). (1988). *Building a professional culture in schools.* New York: Teachers College Press.

Maeroff, G. I. (1988). *The empowerment of teachers: Overcoming the crisis of confidence.* New York: Teachers College Press.

McCall, J. B., & Cousins, J. (1990). *Communication problem solving: The language of effective management.* New York: Wiley.

Morris, W. C., & Sashkin, M. (1976). *Organization behavior in action: Skill building experiences.* St. Paul, MN: West.

Newell, C. (1978). *Human behavior in educational administration.* Englewood Cliffs, NJ: Prentice-Hall.

Olafson, F. A. (1973). *Ethics and twentieth century thought.* Englewood Cliffs, NJ: Prentice-Hall.

Pajak, E. (1989). *The central office supervisor of curriculum and instruction.* Boston, MA: Allyn & Bacon.

Plunkett, L. C., & Hale, G. A. (1982). *The proactive manager: The complete book of problem solving and decision making.* New York: Wiley-Interscience.

Sanderson, M. (1979). *Successful problem management.* New York: Wiley.

Sandole, D. J., & Sandole-Staroste, I. (Eds.). (1987). *Conflict management and problem solving: Interpersonal to international applications.* New York: New York University Press.

Sergiovanni, T. J. (1991). *The principalship: A reflective practice perspective* (2nd ed.). Boston, MA: Allyn & Bacon.

Tanner, D., and Tanner, L. (1987). *Supervision in education: Problems and practices.* New York: Macmillan.

Tarr, G. (1973). *The management of problem-solving: Positive results from productive thinking.* New York: Wiley.

Thomson, S. D. (Ed.). (1993). *Principals for our changing schools: The knowledge and skill base.* Fairfax, VA: National Policy Board for Educational Administration.

Walker, D. (1990). *Fundamentals of curriculum.* New York: Harcourt Brace Jovanovich.

Walker, H. M. (1979). *The acting-out child: Coping with classroom disruption.* Boston, MA: Allyn & Bacon.

Wiles, J., and Bondi, J. (1989). *Curriculum development: A guide to practice* (3rd ed.). New York: Macmillan.

Zais, R. (1976). *Curriculum: Principles and foundation.* New York: Harper Collins.

Chapter

2

......

The Daily Problems of a Middle School Principal

BACKGROUND

F or the following exercises, assume that you are the principal of a 5–8 middle school with 600 students. It is the only middle school in the district. It was built in 1935 as a Works Progress Administration (WPA) project and was first used as the high school for the district. In the early 1960s a new high school was built, and the old high school building became a junior high. In 1982 one of the elementary schools closed because of declining enrollment, and your building became a 5–8 middle school. At times it has been a 7–9 or 6–9 building, depending on demographics. The building is showing its age, but it is structurally sound and has more space than the present student population requires.

The community was a prosperous small city of 35,000 in the mid-1950s. It was a center for furniture manufacture, but all the furniture factories except one have closed. By the late 1970s, the population had fallen by nearly 50%. The most promising of the younger people have long since moved away, leaving the elderly, the undereducated, and the unmotivated behind.

Since the early part of the twentieth century, the city had been predominantly German, Irish, Slovak, and Hungarian. Less than 3% of the community was minority in 1950. In the mid-1970s the state began buying up many of the derelict Victorian mansions just to the east of the decaying central business district and making them halfway houses for drug abusers and first-time offenders. The halfway houses brought many minority people into the area, and many of them chose to stay after being released from their programs. The ethnic composition of the community changed, and minorities, primarily blacks, now make up nearly 30% of the total population and more than 40% of the school population. A significant portion of the black population belongs to the Nation of Islam, and virtually all of the newcomers are from big-city ghettoes.

There has been more and more ethnic tension, but even more problematic than the racial issue has been the clash in values. The conflict surfaced after the 1992 Los Angeles riots and has been evident even to the casual observer ever since. White families have been leaving the community at an accelerated pace. The school board, however, is still all white and has repeatedly been called racist, although no specific allegations have been made.

The black community itself is by no means united. The black population that was here before the mid-1970s has disassociated itself from the recently arrived black population. The Nation of Islam is at odds with the black Christians. There is a black drug subculture and a potent black antidrug group led by Raymond Harris, a Baptist minister. The Hispanic population, approximately 8% of the total population, has been virtually ignored by both the black community and the white community.

The previous principal left to take a principalship in a suburban community some distance away. He told the school board he had begun looking for other positions because he felt that every issue was being made into a racial issue and that his authority had been undermined to the point where he could no longer function effectively. You were selected to replace him precisely because you were a department head in an inner-city high school and had experience dealing with racial issues. You had explained that your situation was very different because there was only a tiny white minority in your old school and the conflicts you faced were divisions among various black groups and among blacks, Hispanics, and Pakistanis. You have been in your present position since July 1.

PROBLEM 14—THE ESSAY CONTEST: WHAT IS ETHNICALLY NEUTRAL?

Every year for as long as anyone can remember, the school board has sponsored a creative writing contest for students in the 5th, 8th, and 11th grades. Because those are the grades in which American history is taught, the theme has always been patriotic. The board has received so much criticism, however, about the racial nature of traditional patriotism, and the judges have had such difficulty evaluating some of the angrier essays, that this year the contest theme was to be dogs. The board felt the topic was neutral and inoffensive.

Shortly after the contest theme was announced, three mothers who said they were representatives of the Black Equality Committee made an appointment to see you. You had never heard of the Black Equality Committee and asked several people, including your superintendent, who they were. No one seemed to know. You resolved to find out.

When the women come for their appointment, you ask what the Black Equality Committee is. They tell you that the group is an unofficial shadow school board that has taken it upon itself to monitor the school board's actions and point out the inequities. They say that they do not feel that the board is intentionally racist, but rather that its members are simply not knowledgeable about the needs of the black community. They intend to support black candidates for the board in the future and to politely but firmly point out inequities to the present board. They say that their aim is to heighten the school system's awareness and strive for equity. As the balance of the school population shifts so that black students are in the majority, they intend to see that the remaining white students are treated fairly.

Their immediate concern is that the announced essay topic is not neutral. They say that the white community sees dogs as family pets and, although some black families have dogs, they are more for protection than for companionship. Most black families live in rental housing where pets are not permitted. Many drug dealers keep attack dogs, trained to be especially vicious, and the other dogs black children hear about are police dogs trained to attack people or sniff out drugs. The committee representatives point out that the black students will realize that the intent of the topic is to have the students write pleasant, funny, or cute stories about pets. They will try to write what they think the judges want to hear, instead of writing from their own experience. Those that do write from their own experience will produce essays far different from what the judges expect, and their essays will therefore not be evaluated fairly.

The women have come to you because two of the three grades for which the contest is being held are in your building, and they feel that you can be instrumental in getting the topic changed to something fair to all students. They hand you a list of topics they think would be fair, thank you for your time, and leave.

The women were polite and correct but cool. It was clear to you that they were evaluating you and that they had planned this meeting very carefully. They remained in charge of it the entire time.

Case Questions

1. What do you intend to do now?

2. In retrospect, should you have taken a more active role in the meeting? You did not because your instincts said that the wisest course was to let them do the talking. Was that a mistake?

3. How would you go about finding out whether the group the women represent is actually influential within the black community?

4. Do you think the women have a valid point?

5. Do you suspect that you will be working with this group in the future? If so, what sort of relationship should you establish with them?

6. What, if anything, do you tell your superintendent about this meeting?

SUGGESTED ACTIVITY: Generate 10 essay topics that are age appropriate and ethnically neutral.

PROBLEM 15—THE NEW POSITION: DETERMINING APPROACH AND SOLUTIONS

The chairperson of the school board phones to inform you that the board has decided to add an additional administrative position to the central office staff. They intend to call the position the minority affairs liaison. The minority affairs liaison will (a) act as a buffer between the administration and the board on one hand and the black community on the other, and (b) advise the administration and the board in their decision making. The salary range for the position is to be the same as for principals.

You are surprised because you had no inkling that anything like this was being considered. The chairperson asks you to serve on a committee to draw up a job description and then to serve on the hiring committee. You listen but do not commit yourself to anything.

Immediately after that conversation, you phone the superintendent, who says that he first heard about the plan this morning. He is concerned because the plan was discussed in secret and without his input. He feels that the new position is a poor idea and is an attempt by the school board to take some of the heat off them. He doubts that the position will serve any useful purpose, and it could exacerbate matters and complicate everything. He told the chairperson that he had reservations about the idea, but he was told that the board had not taken any official action and that the matter was really only being explored. He says that he told the chairperson that the board needed to think the new position out carefully before taking any action. The chairperson said that the board felt that everything should be kept quiet for the moment until there was some agreement on the matter. That is why the superintendent was not consulted and the matter was not discussed in open meeting. Premature disclosure could start a controversy, which would be counterproductive.

The superintendent says he feels that the new position is the chairperson's idea and that there is no support for it among the other board members. His plan is to play a delaying game with the hope that the whole thing will die a natural death. The superintendent tells you to agree to serve on the committee but to drag things out as long as possible without seeming uncooperative.

Case Questions

1. What do you think of the idea of establishing a minority affairs liaison in a district such as this one?
2. If the position is established, how should it fit into the existing administrative structure, and what should the job description be?
3. If the position is established, how will you go about advertising it and screening applicants?
4. What was your immediate reaction when the chairperson informed you of the idea?
5. What do you think about the way the chairperson is handling the matter?
6. What do you think about the superintendent's response?
7. What do you intend to do now?
8. What are your alternative courses of action, and what is the likely outcome of each?
9. What do the chairperson's actions tell you about the way the school board operates?
10. What ethical issues are involved here?

SUGGESTED ACTIVITY: Draw up guidelines of ethical professional behavior to follow when superiors are engaged in behind-the-scenes maneuvering.

PROBLEM 16—THE GIRLS' BASKETBALL COACH: MEETING EVERYONE'S NEEDS

Thomas and Edward Gregg, brothers now in their late 50s, have been the middle-school girls' basketball coaches ever since their daughters were on the team more than 20 years ago. They have done a good job, and no one has given any thought to the fact that they were getting older and might not be available to coach much longer. This past summer Thomas Gregg experienced chest pains. It turned out not to be serious, but recently he came by your office to tell you that his doctor had advised him to slow down. He had always enjoyed coaching and had not thought about retiring from it, but he has decided that it is time to turn the job over to someone younger. His brother Edward says it is time for him to step down too so that a younger person can take over.

In a little less than a month, girls' basketball season begins. The brothers say they are more than willing to work with their replacements but cannot continue coaching even on an interim basis. As soon as you heard that you needed new girls' basketball coaches, you sent a memo out to your faculty asking if anyone was interested. In addition, you talked with the faculty members you considered most likely to be interested, but no one has come forward. You notified the principals in the other schools in the district in case anyone on their staffs wanted to coach the girls. One elementary teacher said that she would be interested in being an assistant coach but didn't feel she could be head coach because she hasn't had the necessary experience. There would be a gap of more than an hour after your dismissal before she could be in your building.

Through further inquiry you find out that the salary for coaching middle school basketball is so low that many people feel it is an insult. The middle school boys' teams have traditionally been a training ground for high school boys' sports, and several people have been willing to coach the boys' teams for that reason. The middle school girls' teams are not viewed in the same way.

Within a few days the news of the coaching opening has spread throughout the community. You have been getting phone calls from people who say it is time you had a black head coach because the majority of the girls' team is black. Other people have been calling to say it is about time you had women coaching the girls' teams. Still others have called to say that, although everyone trusted the Gregg brothers, you had better screen the new applicants carefully. There was a scandal in a nearby district concerning male coaches of girls' teams.

You do not have an athletic director for your school as the high school does. The coaches arrange their own schedules, referees, and transportation. You call the athletic director at the high school. He says that he is hard pressed to find the coaches he needs. He complains that the pay for coaching is so low and the coaches take so much abuse that very few are interested. He suggests that you start by asking the parents of the players.

Case Questions

1. What is the purpose of athletic competition in middle school?
2. What characteristics will you look for in a coach?
3. How will you go about recruiting candidates for the position?
4. How will you screen applicants?
5. Do you want the high school's athletic director to be given responsibility for running your sports programs? Do you want your own athletic director?
6. How will you choose to coordinate your sports programs in the future?
7. What role do you think you should play in your sports programs?

SUGGESTED ACTIVITY: Write out 10 questions to ask of people being interviewed for the coaching position.

PROBLEM 17—THE INTRUSIVE TEACHER: ADJUSTING RELATIONSHIPS

Cheryl Mankin's room is right across the hall from the office. Cheryl is a friendly person who frequently brings in homemade cakes and cookies for the office staff. She is in her mid-30s and unmarried. You often find her in the office talking to your secretaries before and after school. She stays late and often comes in to ask for small things for her room. At first you found her pleasant, but lately you have seen her in the outer office when she should be in the middle of class. When you ask her what she wants, she says she just stopped by because she needs tape or a stapler. You tell her that she should make sure she has what she needs before class begins and that, if some supply is essential in midclass, she should send a student for it. She seems upset that you think she has done anything improper. She says she was out of her room for just a few seconds and she could see and hear what was going on right across the hall.

Cheryl has also taken it upon herself to bring students to the office at lunchtime to decorate the office area with seasonal items. She has a closet in her room filled with decorations she has collected over the years. She is very active in the Parent-Teacher Organization and does volunteer scorekeeping for both the boys' and girls' basketball games. She is also adviser to the school newspaper.

You have begun to notice that, when she is in the office, she automatically answers the phone, deals with people who come in, and helps herself to coffee. About two weeks ago you called her into your office and asked her very tactfully not to come in and take over the secretaries' routine. She said that her only intention was to help out. She became obviously upset, excused herself, and left.

Shortly afterward one of your secretaries came in and said she knew Cheryl could be a bit intrusive but she was a good person with a heart of gold and meant no harm. She went on to say that, since Cheryl had no family, she had made the school her entire life. You responded that at times Cheryl's presence was inappropriate. You appreciated that she did many little things that were thoughtful, but she had overstepped her bounds. You restrained yourself when speaking to your secretary, but you were very annoyed that she was interfering with the way you dealt with a member of the faculty. Your only oral response to that feeling was to say you felt that you had handled the situation correctly. Your secretary seemed by the tone of her voice to have gotten the message. She nodded and left.

You hoped that the matter was closed, and for a few days it seemed to be. In the past two weeks, however, Cheryl has gradually resumed her old behavior patterns. You have just determined that you must take more drastic measures when you see Cheryl come into the office. She sees the parent of one of your students standing there, and she begins to chat. Suddenly you hear her giving the parent confidential information that she could only have gotten from the child's file. The child is not currently one of her students.

Case Questions

1. What steps, if any, do you take immediately?
2. What seems to motivate Cheryl's behavior?
3. What long-range plan will you use to work with Cheryl?
4. How do you deal with your secretaries regarding their relationship to Cheryl?
5. Are there any other issues you must work out with your secretaries?
6. How do you impress on your staff the need to keep confidential information confidential?

SUGGESTED ACTIVITY: Describe in no more than two pages how the main office should be run.

PROBLEM 18—THE CHURCH OF THE ETERNAL LIGHT: SEPARATION OF CHURCH AND STATE

Two years ago Rev. Raymond Harris's church burned to the ground. There was some talk at the time that drug dealers had set the fire as a warning that the Reverend Mr. Harris should stop his antidrug campaign, but there was no evidence to support that theory. Shortly after the fire, the school board gave Mr. Harris permission to use your school for services until his church could be rebuilt. The insurance on the church had not been increased to keep up with inflation, and subsequent fundraisers have fallen far short of expectations. The church has raised only 60% of the money it needs for reconstruction.

Mr. Harris continues to hold services in the cafeteria every Wednesday night and Sunday. The church pays a small fee for utilities, but the janitorial fee has been waived because the congregation cleans the facilities when they are through. The church pays no other fees for the use of your building. So far no one has complained about the arrangement, and there have been no problems. All the arrangements were made long before you were hired, but you have been told of them.

You just received a letter from Mr. Harris in which he asks if he may put a small sign outside the cafeteria entrance to your school to indicate the time of worship and the name of the church. You fear that the request may indicate that the church has no intention of rebuilding in the foreseeable future. The school board did not establish any time by which the church had to move to other facilities. The Reverend Mr. Harris is a respected leader of the black community.

Case Questions

1. Under what circumstances may a church legally use a school building for worship?
2. How will you respond to the letter?
3. If the school board or the superintendent asks what you think should be done about the arrangement with the church, what will you say?

4. If someone is injured during Sunday worship, will the school be liable?

5. If, as a result of Mr. Harris's request, the school board decides to terminate the arrangement with the church, what, if anything, can you do to maintain a good working relationship with Mr. Harris?

6. What sort of relationships should a principal have with community leaders? With religious leaders?

SUGGESTED ACTIVITY: Find out what the legal restrictions are on the use of a school as a place of worship during nonschool hours.

PROBLEM 19—THE PARAPLEGIC STUDENT: ACCOMMODATING SPECIAL-NEEDS STUDENTS

Part 1—Sandra's History

Sandra Crawford was a very athletic girl. Last summer she dove from a bridge into a river, hit the bottom with considerable force, and suffered a severe spinal injury. She is permanently paralyzed from the waist down. Since the accident, Sandra has been in the hospital and then in a facility for convalescence and physical therapy. She will be returning to school soon. She has kept up with her schoolwork through tutors, who have been teaching her all her subjects on site.

Sandra is a seventh-grader, and seventh-graders normally change classes every period. You have a two-story building with a gym at a level lower than the first floor. In recent years ramps have been built to make the gym and the first floor wheelchair-accessible from the outside, but there is no elevator, and many of Sandra's classes are on the second floor. In addition, to reach the gym by wheelchair from the first floor, one must go outside the building. There are bathrooms on the first floor that are equipped for use by the physically handicapped. Sandra will be the first permanently wheelchair-bound student in your building. In the past, special arrangements have been made for physically handicapped students, but those students had temporary conditions or lesser handicaps.

The chairperson of the school board, Mrs. Borden, has said that the thing to do is to move all the classes Sandra has to the first floor and to make sure that next year all the eighth-grade classes will be on the first floor. The primary difficulty in moving classrooms is that the science rooms are all on the second floor. If the seventh-grade science classes were moved to the first floor, the teacher's ability to provide laboratory experiences would be severely limited. The library is also on the second floor, and there does not seem to be any way to make that facility accessible to Sandra.

Architecturally there is no easy solution to the problem of internal access to the gym. The stairs are steep and there is not sufficient room to build a ramp long enough to have the required slope. Mrs. Borden suggested building a covered walkway from the wheelchair-accessible main entrance to the external gym entrance. The only other mandated requirement would be to change some of the doors to allow wheelchairs to enter. There is absolutely no money for putting in elevators, and because of the way the gym was added, there would have to be two elevators, one for access to the gym and one for access to the second floor. Also, a bathroom equipped for the physically handicapped would have to be built on the second floor, and showers and toilets for the handicapped would have to be added to the locker rooms.

The chairperson pointed out that by the time a bond issue was voted on and the modifications were made, Sandra would be in high school. There do not appear to be any permanently wheelchair-bound students in the elementary program, and it is impractical for the impoverished system to pay enormous amounts of money to make modifications for just one student, even if much of the cost would be covered by the state. The covered walkway, the door modifications, and the moving of classrooms would be very expensive as it was. There was no money in the budget for such expenditures. Having Sandra return to school would certainly push the district into debt. If possible, the chairperson would like to have the district pay the tuition for Sandra to attend some other facility for middle school. The high school is already equipped to handle handicapped students.

Mrs. Borden has long advocated building a new middle school. There have been several unsuccessful attempts over the past eight years to pass a bond issue to build the new school. She says that if the system is forced to make major renovations for Sandra, all hope of a new facility, which would include handicapped access, will be lost.

Mrs. Borden has come into your office to speak to you privately. She wants you to tell her frankly what you think about her plan to accommodate Sandra. She also wants you to go to the Crawfords' home and find out how they would feel about having Sandra's tuition paid to another facility.

Case Questions

1. What must you do legally to accommodate Sandra?
2. Mrs. Borden has bypassed the central office and come directly to you with this matter. What does that mean? What should you do about it?
3. How do you deal with Mrs. Borden now that she is in your office?
4. What do you think of Mrs. Borden's plan to pay to send Sandra to an out-of-district school?
5. If the superintendent asked you to approach Sandra's parents with the suggestion that the district pay Sandra's tuition to another school for the remainder of her middle-school education, how would you respond?

Part 2—Outside Agencies Become Involved

Various plans for Sandra's education have been proposed to the Crawfords. They have listened attentively and have indicated that they are willing to consider having Sandra sent to a neighboring district's middle school. You are awaiting their response when a representative of an advocacy group for the handicapped comes into your office and informs you that, if you fail to provide for Sandra appropriately in your building, the district, the superintendent, the school board members, and you personally will be sued. You phone the Crawfords and find out that they had decided to have Sandra sent to the other school if your district would also provide transportation in both directions when someone from the advocacy group contacted them and said that Sandra would be harmed if she were not allowed to rejoin her classmates in the school she had a legal right to attend. The head of the advocacy group said that they would take over the fight for Sandra now. The Crawfords were confused and didn't know what was the best thing to do for their daughter.

Case Questions

1. What do you do now?
2. How do you protect yourself and your district?
3. What do you think would be the best thing for Sandra?
4. How, in general, do you deal with special interest groups?
5. What do you think is the likely outcome of this situation?

SUGGESTED ACTIVITY: Find out what the courts in your state have required schools to do recently to meet the needs of the handicapped.

PROBLEM 20—THE QUESTION OF ATTEMPTED RAPE: DETERMINING THE LIMITS OF RESPONSIBILITY

You are just ready to go home for the day when Mrs. Brown comes into your office. She is working hard to control herself but is obviously upset. You have her take a seat and ask her what the problem is. She says that on the way home from school her daughter Tanya, a seventh-grader, stopped at the public library. Two of her classmates, Michael O'Brien and Edward Schmidt, were also in the library. They followed Tanya around and began annoying her. Then they started making obscene suggestions. Tanya got scared and ran out of the library to her home. The boys followed her and caught up with her in the foyer of Tanya's apartment building. The boys pinned Tanya up against the mailboxes. Tanya started screaming. Mrs. Brown ran out into the hall and saw the boys run out the door. Tanya was shaking uncontrollably and sobbing. Her panties had been pulled down around her ankles. When she calmed down enough to speak, she said that the boys had tried to rape her. Mrs. Brown wants you to expel both boys immediately. She says that her daughter is a good Christian girl and that she will not tolerate this sort of behavior.

Case Questions

1. How do you respond to Mrs. Brown?
2. What responsibility does the school have for the behavior of its students when they are off school grounds?

3. Can the school, the district, or you be held legally responsible for the actions of the students on their way to and from school?

4. How would you go about investigating the incident?

5. Tanya is black, and Michael and Edward are white. In a school where race relations are precarious, what steps might you take to keep the incident from triggering further racial tension and conflict?

6. If, in your investigation of the incident, it appears that Mrs. Brown's account is accurate, what do you do?

7. Suppose that, in your investigation of the incident, Edward and Michael claim that Tanya stole Michael's Walkman and they chased her home to get it back. Suppose they say that, if Tanya's panties were pulled down, she pulled them down herself to accuse them of attempted rape and cover up her theft. What do you do?

8. Do you report the incident to the police? If so, at what point?

SUGGESTED ACTIVITY: Investigate current legal opinion concerning a school's off-campus responsibilities to students.

PROBLEM 21—THE ALTERNATIVE SCHOOL PROGRAM: EVALUATING IDEAS AND DETERMINING FUTURE ACTIONS

The standardized test results have been dropping steadily districtwide. A group of parents, predominantly white, have gotten together with some of the members of the school board and are now proposing that the schools admit that the traditional programs are simply not effective with an identifiable group of students. They say the school board needs to admit that there is no one appropriate way to educate all students and that the disaffected students should be given a totally different type of education. The group has done some preliminary research on alternative school programs of the past, particularly the 1970s, and has discovered that several models were consistently successful. Many of the programs were discontinued, not because they didn't work, but rather because they ceased to be in vogue and receive funding. What the group is suggesting now is that an official committee be established to investigate the possibility of establishing an alternative middle-school program for capable but disaffected students.

When the proposal was brought before the entire school board, it met with mixed reaction. Some people said that students had to learn to cope with the standard program because it was designed to prepare them for the real world. Others said they had no desire to return to the excesses and failed experiments of the past. A third group said that there was simply no money to operate such a program, no matter what its merits. The programs in the 1970s had been run on federal grant money, which has since disappeared. Finally, a Hispanic woman in the audience stood up and said that the suggestion was simply a disguised way to shunt minorities into substandard programs. At that point, discussion became heated, and it took several minutes for the chairperson to get the meeting back to order.

One of the members of the school board who had kept silent during the discussion said that the basis of the concern was real and that it would be foolish to dismiss the suggestion of an alternative school program without exploring the possibility of outside funding and trying to work through the objections. That member said that the matter should be explored more carefully and suggested that a small ad hoc committee be established to look into the possibility more fully. A motion to that effect was made, seconded, and passed quickly. The chairperson asked two parents from the original group of concerned parents, the Hispanic woman from the audience, the member of the school board who had proposed the committee, and you to form such an ad hoc committee and report back to the board in one month. The superintendent said nothing during the entire exchange.

Case Questions

1. What do you think was the real intent of the school board member who proposed the committee?
2. Do you think the concept is worth pursuing? Why or why not?
3. How do you respond?
4. What role should you play as a member of the committee?
5. How do you interpret the superintendent's silence on the matter?
6. What do you think will come of the idea?

SUGGESTED ACTIVITY: Describe how you would investigate both the proposal itself and the political base from which it arose.

PROBLEM 22—THE CRACK PIPE: DEALING WITH SUBSTANCE ABUSE

Part 1—Opening Pandora's Box

After late basketball practice one afternoon, Steve Marion, an eighth-grader, comes into your office and tells you that he just found a crack pipe in the parking lot right next to a red pickup with the license plate NHJ 348. He hands you the pipe, and you ask him exactly how he found it. He says that he left the building by the side door to wait for his brother to pick him up. When his brother pulled in, Steve saw an object reflecting the car's headlights. He went over and picked it up. When he saw what it was, he brought it directly to you. The pipe was on the ground right in front of the driver's door of the pickup. He says he has to go because his brother is waiting, and he leaves. Steve has always been a dependable student and a good kid.

On a hunch you check the license plate numbers listed on the employees' parking sticker applications. Just as you suspected, Ralph Walsh is the owner of the pickup. Ralph is the son of one of the members of the board of education. You know he had the reputation of being a wild kid, he flunked out of college, and he was given a job as janitor because your predecessor thought that might straighten him out.

Case Questions

1. What do you do now?
2. What will you say to Steve Marion when you see him in the morning?
3. What are your legal and ethical obligations to Ralph, to the students in your building, and to the district?

SUGGESTED ACTIVITY: Find out your district's policy regarding substance abuse among employees.

Part 2—The Task Force

Word of the crack pipe found near Ralph Walsh's truck spread rapidly throughout the district. You were very careful to keep the matter confidential, but any one or all of several people could have spread the story. Within an hour of the discovery, the superintendent called you to say that Ralph had resigned. The furor did not die. The school guidance counselor decided it was time to form an anti-substance-abuse task force, briefly mentioned the idea to you, and went ahead with the formation of the group. Steve Marion and some other student athletes were recruited to be on the task force, as were Rev. Raymond Harris and the school nurse. You were to be an ex officio member of the task force, which would meet after school on Thursdays.

You attended the first meeting and presented several ideas you had already been working on. Your ideas centered on bringing in several outside speakers and experienced drug counselors. The news that you were already working on the problem was received warmly, but Mr. Harris said that the school and the community were already at or near the crisis stage and that such approaches could not work by themselves. The group brainstormed various ways to get across the message that alcohol and other drugs were uncool and dangerous. The students were fully involved and enthusiastic. You left the meeting feeling that your efforts were being supported and that something good might come out of the group.

During the next few meetings, various ideas emerged, such as peer counseling and referral services, stiffer antidrug policies, and participation in a statewide anti-substance-abuse network. You could not be present for the entire meeting every week, but you dropped in as you could. The group seemed to be getting beyond its initial overenthusiasm and becoming a real working organization. You have worked with the group to implement some of their ideas and have explained why others could not be used or required training, other preparation, or school board approval before implementation. You have felt comfortable with the way things were going. Even the superintendent has commended the task force.

One day nearly two months after the formation of the task force, Steve Marion asks to speak with you privately. He says that James Franklin, a 16-year-old eighth-grader, is selling drugs out of his locker. James keeps a pile of old sweat socks, half-eaten sandwiches, and other debris in the bottom of his locker to hide his stash. Steve also says that Rachael Mason's older sister sells alcohol to the middle school students from the trunk of her car, which she parks just around the corner from the front of the building. He goes on to say that either Richy Levitt or Lamont Stevenson was selling uppers to the seventh-graders in the cafeteria boys' room during lunch. He says that Sandra Thomas keeps her thermos filled with screwdrivers and that Bob Evens, a sixth-grader, got so drunk last Saturday night that he passed out in the rest room of the Exxon station on Maple Street and would have drowned in his own vomit if a motorist hadn't stopped in to use the facilities at just the right time.

Case Questions

1. What do you do with the information Steve has reported to you about each of the situations?
2. What sort of relationship should a middle-school principal have with the police in cases of substance abuse among students?
3. What are the laws of search and seizure as applied to a principal's actions?
4. How will you now deal with Steve and the task force?
5. What are your legal, moral, and ethical concerns when presented with this information?
6. What are the consequences likely to be if you do nothing with the information given you?

Part 3—The Nurse's Concerns

Later, on the same day Steve Marion came to you with his information, the school nurse comes into your office. She says that at the end of the last few meetings, after you left, the task force degenerated into a sort of conspiracy of informants. The entire last meeting, which you missed, was nothing but gossip about who was suspected of doing what. She is sure at least some of the information was wrong or made up because the atmosphere of the meeting was such that students were trying to outdo each other with their revelations. She wants you to dissolve the task force. She wants no further part of it.

Case Questions

1. What will you do with the task force now?
2. Can you allow a group of student informants to operate in your school?
3. What message will you be sending out if you dissolve the task force?

4. Can you refocus the group?
5. How do you deal with the nurse?

SUGGESTED ACTIVITY: Write a two- to three-page paper in which you (a) discuss the role, composition, structure, and scope a site-based substance-abuse-prevention committee should have, and (b) state and defend your reason for electing to support or not to support the creation of such a committee in your school.

PROBLEM 23—MALCOLM X: THE UNAUTHORIZED CURRICULUM

Ms. Tshombe, an eighth-grade U.S. history teacher, has been an active member of the Nation of Islam for some time. She is a strict disciplinarian and has the reputation of being a good teacher. You have noted, from the lesson plans she hands in every week, that she should now be teaching western expansion, urbanization, industrialization, and immigration. You happen to stop by her room and find that she is talking about Malcolm X. It is February, and you assume that she is taking some time to honor Black American History Month. The class seems to be productive. About a week later you happen by her room again and see that she is still teaching about Malcolm X. That afternoon you ask one of the students from her fifth-period class what the class has been studying. The student says that Ms. Tshombe has been talking about Malcolm X for almost three weeks and that this Friday evening she is taking a group of students to a mosque in a nearby city. None of that is in the lesson plans she submitted to you. The student says that Ms. Tshombe covered western expansion, immigration, urbanization, and the growth of industry in one class a long time ago. You are amazed that you haven't had any parent complaints about the nature of the instruction in this class if what this student says is true.

Case Questions

1. How will you investigate this matter?
2. What do you do in general when a teacher deviates substantially from the approved curriculum?
3. How will you deal with the upcoming field trip to the mosque?
4. How will you deal with the deception Ms. Tshombe has apparently attempted by turning in lesson plans that do not reflect what she is teaching?
5. How do you feel about establishing an Afrocentric curriculum?

SUGGESTED ACTIVITY: Describe how you would investigate and document this situation, and write out the steps you would take to monitor the curriculum within your school.

PROBLEM 24—JASON: THE DRASTIC CHANGE

Harry Mercer is a second-year eighth-grade English teacher who has come to your office after school seeking advice. It is mid-October, and something about Jason Larkins is bothering him. On the surface Jason dresses, talks, and acts like the stereotypic 13-year-old boy. He often does not hand in homework, he goofs off in class, and at times he seems almost to want to be assigned detentions. He earns poor to average grades, but something about his work distinguishes it from that of the typical mediocre student. Even though he sees Jason only 45 minutes a day, Harry's senses tell him that something about Jason is phony. He has asked his colleagues who had Jason last year, and they tell him that Jason was a model student who got top grades. Harry says that he understands that middle-school students often try out different personalities, styles of dress, and ways of acting to impress their peers or gain acceptance and as a part of growing up. Harry says that he had anticipated that Jason would get tired of sabotaging his own work and would revert to his normal pattern. It is now the end of the seventh week of school, and Jason is maintaining his performance. Harry went to the guidance counselor, where he learned that last week Jason dropped out of Algebra I and is now taking Math 8. Harry says that Jason's pretense has gone on long enough, and he wants your help to put an end to it.

Case Questions

1. Do you find substance in Harry's concerns?
2. Should the school do something about Jason at this point?
3. At what point does adolescent experimenting become a problem?
4. Should the parents be involved?
5. What advice do you give Harry?
6. Is it important to know Jason's ethnic background to determine how to deal with this problem? Why or why not?

SUGGESTED ACTIVITY: Find out what research indicates about students who purposely underachieve.

PROBLEM 25—THE FLASHERS: A QUESTION OF PROPER SUPERVISION

Part 1—A Problem Is Exposed

To comply with Title IX regulations, your school has long alternated game and practice times for the eighth-grade boys' and girls' basketball teams. On days with even-numbered dates, the girls practice first while the boys wait in the cafeteria, and on the other days, the boys get the gym first. By contract, the coaches have to supervise their teams in the cafeteria until their turn to use the gym. Because having unsupervised students in the building for long periods can create problems, all team members have to report to either the gym or the cafeteria within five minutes of the end of the school day. The group in the cafeteria is required to do homework or read quietly. Today it is the girls' turn to have first practice, so the boys are in the cafeteria.

Earlier this afternoon, Brad Flemming, the boys' coach, had to transfer funds from his savings account to his checking account to cover his mortgage payment. He saw Sandra Crowley going past the cafeteria on her way out of the building. He ran after her and asked if she would watch his team long enough for him to go to the bank. He estimated that it would take no more than 15 minutes. She agreed to cover for him. Without going back into the cafeteria, Coach Flemming left for the bank. Ms. Crowley went into the cafeteria and began correcting papers as she supervised the students. Coach Flemming came back in 15 minutes, as he had said he would, thanked Ms. Crowley, and resumed supervision. Ms. Crowley left the building immediately, after telling Coach Flemming that the boys had all been quiet. A few minutes after Ms. Crowley left, Coach Flemming noticed that Willie Sandman and Bruce Plesser were not among the students in the cafeteria. He knew that those two boys were great pranksters and immediately began to search for them.

He did not have to search long. The girls had just finished practice and walked past the cafeteria on their way to their locker room. Moments later Coach Flemming heard a loud commotion from that part of the building. Then he saw Monica Brown, a science teacher in your building and the newly appointed girls' coach, dragging Willie and Bruce, both totally naked except for their sneakers, from the girls' locker room to the cafeteria. Willie looked scared, but Bruce's face was contorted.

Coach Brown said the two boys had stripped and had hidden in the girls' locker room. Once most of the girls had entered the room, the boys sprang from their hiding place and flashed the girls. They thought to make their escape but literally ran into Coach Brown just as they were about to exit the locker room. She grabbed them by their arms and dragged them roughly down the hall to the cafeteria, still naked. It was later discovered that the boys had disrobed and stored their clothes in the boys' locker room, whose entrance was about 10 feet from the girls'.

Coach Brown berated Coach Flemming for not supervising his team properly. Bruce began to cry and beg Coach Brown to let him go. She released him. Brad Flemming angrily asked Monica Brown why she hadn't had them cover themselves before she dragged them through the hall. Coach Brown said that since the boys apparently liked to be naked she couldn't be bothered saving them the embarrassment they had brought on themselves. She added that they had practically nothing to cover anyway.

By then a large group of people had gathered around the entrance to the cafeteria. You are among the last to arrive. You are about to ask what happened when you see the two naked boys. You demand that they be given something to wear immediately. Someone finds towels for Willie and Bruce. You tell Coach Brown to go back to the girls' locker room and supervise her team. You tell the onlookers to disperse, the boys except for Willie and Bruce to suit up for practice, and Coach

Flemming to tell you what happened. He tells you about having to go to the bank and having Ms. Crowley cover for him. Willie confesses that, as soon as the coach had left the cafeteria to ask Ms. Crowley to supervise while he went to the bank, they sneaked out and went into the boys' locker room, where they devised the plan to expose themselves to the girls.

Bruce now sinks to the floor and begins sobbing and holding his arm. You ask him what the matter is. Bruce says his arm and shoulder hurt more than anything has ever hurt him before.

You tell Coach Flemming to go to the boys' locker room and tell his team to report back to the cafeteria once they have suited up. You stay with Bruce and Willie. Willie complains that Coach Brown had no cause to treat them the way she did. Maybe they shouldn't have done what they did, but she shouldn't have either. They are just kids and only meant to have a little fun, but she is a teacher.

As soon as Coach Flemming returns from delivering his message, you tell him to have Willie dress in his school clothes and report to your office. You tell the coach to stay with Bruce and the rest of his team in the cafeteria. On your way back to your office, you stop by the girls' locker room and tell Coach Brown to report to your office as soon as the last of the girls finish changing.

Case Questions

1. What do you think of Coach Flemming's behavior? Coach Brown's? Yours?
2. Did Ms. Crowley do anything improper? What responsibility did she take on when she agreed to supervise the team in the cafeteria?
3. What should you do now with regard to Bruce, Willie, Coach Brown, and Coach Flemming? What should you do as soon as you return to your office?
4. What should Coach Flemming do now with Bruce and the rest of his team?

Part 2—The Dislocated Shoulder

Shortly after 9:00 that evening, the superintendent calls to tell you that he has been notified that Bruce has a dislocated shoulder and his parents intend to sue the school. He asks you for written accounts from all personnel involved, describing in detail what happened. He expects the accounts in his office by the end of the day tomorrow. You call Coach Brown, Coach Flemming, and Ms. Crowley to tell them to prepare detailed written reports of the incident and have them in your office by the beginning of school the next day. You immediately start writing your own description of the incident. You are disturbed because Coach Brown sounded hostile on the phone and Ms. Crowley was upset.

Case Questions

1. Do you think that Bruce's parents have solid grounds for pressing legal suit? If so, against whom and on what grounds?

2. What should you do regarding the statements the superintendent requested? How should you prepare your own statement? What advice if any should you give your teachers?

3. Is the time allotted for the preparation of the statements realistic?

4. What do you expect each of the statements to contain?

5. Was it a good idea to require each party involved to write such a statement? If you were the superintendent, what would you do with the statements?

6. What should you do now regarding Bruce, Willie, Coach Brown, Ms. Crowley, Coach Flemming, and the basketball teams?

SUGGESTED ACTIVITY: Without looking back at the case, write a statement concerning the incident, as the superintendent requested. Now compare the facts in your statement with the facts given in the case.

PROBLEM 26—THE BANK ROBBER: DEALING WITH REACTION

Today, February 11, the back doors of the school were propped open because the custodians were in the middle of unloading a delivery of paper supplies. Very suddenly a man in a ski mask rushed through the open door, carrying a rifle and a large canvas pouch. The custodians dropped the cartons they were off-loading, jumped into the cab of the delivery truck with the driver, and sped off. Once they were a safe distance from the school, the driver radioed the police to tell them that an armed man had entered the building.

By the time the police phone you, you have heard the news from a music teacher, who saw the man with the rifle, locked her door, evacuated her students through a window, and brought her class around the building to the office. You have contacted the teachers in rooms 12 and 112 via intercom, instructing them to close and chain the fire doors outside their rooms. You have run down to the gym, entering through the outside doors. You have evacuated all the students to the outside and then to the main part of the building. To the best of your knowledge, the armed man is now isolated in the west wing. You have just ordered all the outside doors shut and locked and have ordered everyone in the building to lie flat on the floor and stay there. You tell the police what you have done. They ask you to check with each of your teachers to find out if anyone is hurt and to make sure all students are accounted for. You find that three students are unaccounted for but that no one is hurt. By this time a SWAT team has surrounded the building.

Sylvia Montefiore, a part-time Chapter II teacher, drives into the parking lot, gets out of her car, and taps one of the SWAT officers on the shoulder, asking if she should enter the building. The officer throws Ms. Montefiore to the ground, tearing and soiling her coat. She is very angry, but just then there is an exchange of gunfire, and the police storm the west wing. The armed man is killed. It is later confirmed that the man was fleeing after robbing a bank two blocks away.

The police do a complete search of the building. They find the three missing students hiding in lockers in the boys' locker room. They had cut class to play poker, and when they heard you evacuate the gym, they decided to hide in the lockers. They say the robber never even came into the locker room. There is several thousand dollars' damage to the west wing as a result of the gunfight, but no one associated with the school was hurt except for Ms. Montefiore, who hurt her knee. She is now loudly demanding that the school pay for her ruined coat.

You report everything to the superintendent, who asks you to get the school day started tomorrow and, once things have returned as nearly to normal as possible, to come to his office. He advises you just to finish up at school as best you can today and go home and unwind.

The police and reporters are all over the school. The phones have been ringing incessantly, mostly with calls from parents who want to make sure their children are OK. It is after 8:00 when you finally get home. You disconnect the phone, have supper, take a long bath, and fall asleep in front of the television while watching an old movie.

The next morning everyone in the building seems to have some vivid story about his or her role in the adventure, but by the end of first period, the excitement appears to have subsided to a reasonable level, and you leave for the superintendent's office. The superintendent says that, since you refused to answer the phone last night, everyone called him. Although he was not pleased, he could understand that, by the time you got home, you needed to unwind. He says the only reason people didn't go to your house last night or approach you first thing this morning is that he asked everyone to give you breathing space and told them that he would be working with you now to resolve all the issues. Those issues are as follows:

1. How could three students get away with sneaking off to the locker room to play poker? The boys had confessed that it was not the first time they had succeeded in sneaking off.
2. What security measures are needed to make the building safe?
3. What if the robber had already fled into the main part of the building when you ordered the doors secured? You might have trapped him in a whole school full of hostages.
4. What, if anything, do you intend to do to deal with the residual effect of the incident among the students and staff? Do you think everything is now resolved?
5. How do you plan to allay the parents' fears about the safety of their children?

Before you even have a chance to reply, the superintendent tells you that there will be a special school board meeting tomorrow night to give you a chance to describe the entire incident, respond to the issues he has mentioned, and answer any questions. He says that he has asked you to his office to give you a chance to work out your plans and write a statement to be released to the press. That statement should serve as the groundwork for tomorrow night's meeting. He also wants you to find a way to keep "that stupid Montefiore woman" off his back. When you have worked things out in your mind and have prepared the statement, he will listen to your plan and read your statement. Then you will be free to go back to your building. With that he leaves you to your task.

Case Questions

1. List and analyze your actions during the crisis and afterwards.
2. What legal issues are likely to arise as a result of this crisis?
3. What should be done about the three boys who were cutting class?
4. How can you best handle the problem of cutting classes?
5. Is there anything more you can do with regard to the reactions of the faculty and the students to the crisis?
6. What is your opinion of the actions of your custodians?
7. What do you think of the way the superintendent is handling this situation?
8. How do you respond to the issues raised by the superintendent?
9. How do you plan to prepare for the school board meeting tomorrow night?
10. How will you deal with Ms. Montefiore and her coat?
11. How will you deal with the superintendent?

SUGGESTED ACTIVITY: Write the press release requested by the superintendent.

CHAPTER SUMMARY

In a small city with a declining population and rapidly shifting demographics, all professionals must be aware that the people who have remained when the sources of employment have shrunk are those who have seniority in their places of work, those who have retired, those with very strong ties to the area, and those without the ambition, training, or the education to seek out places that might offer better opportunities. People who have retired or who have a great deal of seniority are unlikely to have school-aged children or a great stake in the quality of the schools. Many of their children have already moved out of the area. In addition, communities with long-term unemployment often foster an atmosphere of hopelessness or low expectations. Such communities frequently look shabby and inadvertently discourage regeneration. Such negative attitudes may be reflected very clearly in the schools.

It is essential in such locations for educational leaders to create the most positive possible school climate, beginning by keeping the physical plant as clean and attractive as possible. In cities in decline, the school buildings are usually old and in need of constant attention. Resources in such instances are almost always scarce. Despite the age of the buildings, and even with limited resources, volunteer student and community labor can, if contractual, union, and insurance obstacles are cleared, be used to enhance what is there so that people can take pride in their schools.

Rapidly changing demographics usually have the effect of bringing racial or ethnic concerns into every aspect of life. In such a setting, tension and territoriality are virtually always present, and friction is often just below the surface. Administrators at all levels must consider those characteristics when making decisions. The ethnic background of the principal will be a factor in his or her ability to implement certain solutions to problems.

In the situation described in this chapter, there are two major competing groups, blacks and whites. For the moment, ethnic differences within each group seem to have been put aside, and racial identification is much stronger than it might otherwise be. The true minority group here is the Hispanics. Because they represent such a small part of the total population, their needs may be overlooked. It is essential for administrators to deal fairly with all segments of the school population and to be especially sensitive toward small minority groups.

In such settings the purpose of education must also be reexamined. If we educate students well, we ensure that many of the most capable students will leave the area and loosen their bonds with their families and community. It is painful for parents to realize that for their children to flourish they must move away. Some parents may even be willing to sacrifice their children's futures to keep the children nearby. We must also be aware that we may be preparing the people who will lead the area out of its decline.

The middle school is the stepchild of the educational system. By the time students reach middle school, their parents are no longer as involved with the schools as they were in the lower grades. Middle school lacks the sentimental attachment and glamour high schools and high school sports and activities call to mind. Most people look back fondly on their childhood and later adolescence. Preadolescence and puberty bring about such awkward changes that few of us care to dwell on our memories of them. Not many people would care to be 13 again or to be surrounded by 13-year-olds. Middle schools now have all the problems high schools had 20 years ago, and the students lack the appeal of younger children.

Many teachers and administrators take middle-school positions with the intention of moving to a high school as soon as there is an appropriate opening. What is often overlooked is that during this difficult time of life, good teachers can have a tremendous impact on their students. It is a time when avocational interests are often developed and when attitudes and behaviors are usually shaped that will carry students into independence and adulthood. Middle school is usually the last real chance students have to make up skill deficiencies. It is important that administrators at this level do as much as possible to make sure their staffs appreciate the educational opportunities and challenges they have and to encourage faculty who really wish to teach at a different level to find positions suitable to them.

There can be no question that our surroundings influence our reactions. Even when we try to stay aloof from our environment, over time it cannot help influence the way we see the world. Most people are knowledgeable about the settings they function in. Many consciously take that knowledge into account when making decisions. The difficulty is knowing how to use that knowledge. In a community in decline, it seems natural to adjust standards of both behavior and academic performance downward. That adjustment, often made subconsciously, may simply contribute to the downward spiral of the community's decline. How to use professional insights about the community is an extremely complex question. It is essential that educators periodically examine the specifics of setting and scrutinize the impact the setting can and should have on their functioning and decision making.

In this chapter you have been faced with problems that concern, among other things, the separation of church and state, race relations, minorities, handicapped students, puberty, violence in the community, and increased involvement with the school board. It is important that you examine your thoughts, opinions, and feelings about each of those issues. Administrators need to have such issues resolved in their own minds so that they can act without bringing personal baggage into play. Use the cases to reflect on your beliefs concerning the issues the problems revolve around.

Some of the questions we have explored in this chapter have far greater legal implications than the ones posed in Chapter 1. To be certified, most administrators must take at least one course in school law. Difficulties arise for administrators who fail to recognize that the law is constantly evolving and that what is true at one time will most likely not remain true forever. If we are trapped into thinking that, by virtue of our training, we can anticipate the legal ramifications of particular actions, we may be in for a rude awakening. The areas of student and teacher rights, the rights of the handicapped, and church–school relations are changing particularly rapidly. When you deal with problems in legally sensitive areas, it is important to know how and when to seek a legal opinion. Virtually all school districts retain legal counsel, but the advice of such counsel is expensive and must be used wisely.

SUGGESTED ACTIVITY: Reconsider your approach to each of the problems in this chapter. For which ones, if any, should you seek legal counsel, and how do you make that determination?

SUMMARY QUESTIONS

1. What special concerns does an administrator have in a school whose ethnic composition is changing rapidly?

2. From what little you have been told about the superintendent, what sort of person do you think he is? What type of relationship would you choose to establish with him?

3. Do you see this principalship as a high-stress position? If so, how would you deal with that stress?

4. Given the opportunity, how important is it to you to bring more minority people into the faculty? Why?

5. Do you think a school undergoing this type of transition requires a more authoritarian administrator than the elementary school described in Chapter 1? Why or why not?

SUGGESTED READING

Alexander, K., & Alexander, M. D. (1984). *The law of schools, students, and teachers in a nutshell.* St. Paul, MN: West.

Arnold, J. D. (1992). *The complete problem solver: A total system for competitive decision making.* New York: Wiley.

Blumberg, A., & Greenfield, W. (1980). *The effective principal: Perspectives on school leadership.* Boston, MA: Allyn & Bacon.

Carew, J. V., & Lightfoot, S. L. (1979). *Beyond bias: Perspectives on classrooms.* Cambridge, MA: Harvard University Press.

Cookson, P. W., Sadovnik, A. R., & Semel, S. F. (1992). *International handbook of educational reform.* Westport, CT: Greenwood Press.

Darder, A. (1991). *Culture and power in the classroom: A critical foundation for bicultural education.* Westport, CT: Bergin & Garvey.

Dunn, K.J., & Dunn, R. S. (Eds.). (1983). *Situational leadership for principals: The school administrator in action.* Englewood Cliffs, NJ: Prentice-Hall.

Etzione, A. (1991). Social science as a mulitcultural canon. *Society, 29*(1), 14–18.

Garcia, E. E. (1993). America's changing demographics: Educational policy implications. *Education and Urban Society, 25*(3), 270–284.

Genck, F. H. (1991). *Renewing America's progress: A positive solution to school reform.* Westport, CT: Praeger.

Guthrie, J., & Reed, R. (1986). *Educational administration and policy.* Englewood Cliffs, NJ: Prentice-Hall.

Hoy, W., & Forsyth, P. (1986). *Effective supervision: Theory into practice.* New York: Random House.

Lankard, B. A. (1987). *Accepting responsibility.* Columbus, OH: Ohio State University, National Center for Research in Vocational Education.

Lieberman, A. (Ed.). (1988). *Building a professional culture in schools.* New York: Teachers College Press.

Maeroff, G. I. (1988). *The empowerment of teachers: Overcoming the crisis of confidence.* New York: Teachers College Press.

Olafson, F. A. (1973). *Ethics and twentieth century thought.* Englewood Cliffs, NJ: Prentice-Hall.

O'Reilly, R. C., & Green, E. T. (1992). *School law for the 1990s: A handbook.* Westport, CT: Greenwood Press.

Owens, R. G. (1970). *Organizational behavior in schools.* Englewood Cliffs, NJ: Prentice-Hall.

Pennings, J. M. (1983). *Decision making: An organizational behavioral approach.* New York: M. Wiener.

Rosenhead, J. (Ed.). (1989). *Rational analysis for a problematic world: Problem structuring methods for complexity, uncertainty, and conflict.* New York: Wiley.

Sergiovanni, T. J. (1989). *Moral leadership: Getting to the heart of school improvement.* San Francisco, CA: Jossey-Bass.

Sergiovanni, T. J. (1989). *Schooling for tomorrow: Directing reforms to issues that count.* Boston, MA: Allyn and Bacon.

Sergiovanni, T. J. (1991). *The principalship: A reflective practice perspective* (2nd ed.). Boston, MA: Allyn & Bacon.

Schultz, F. (Ed.). (1994). *Multicultural education 94/95.* Guilford, CT: Dushkin Publishing Group.

Sydoriak, D. (1993). Designing schools for all kids. *Educational facility planner, 31*(5), 15–17.

Sybouts, W. (1992). *Planning in school administration: A handbook.* Westport, CT: Greenwood Press.

Thomson, S. D. (Ed.). (1993). *Principals for our changing schools: The knowledge and skill base.* Fairfax, VA: National Policy Board for Educational Administration.

Ubben, G. C., and Hughes, L. W. (1992). *The principal: Creative leadership for effective schools* (2nd ed.). Boston, MA: Allyn & Bacon.

Webb, L. D., Greer, J. Y., Montello, P. A., & Norton, M. S. (1987). *Personnel administration in education.* Columbus, OH: Merrill.

Yukl, G. (1989). *Leadership in organizations* (2nd ed.). Englewood Cliffs, NJ: Prentice-Hall.

Chapter

3

......

The Daily Problems of a High School Principal

BACKGROUND

F or all the situations presented in this chapter, assume you are the principal of a 9–12 high school. The school is in a district that was created by the U.S. Circuit Court of Appeals during the 1970s. The court combined the school districts in two counties that together comprised the metropolitan area of a medium-sized city. To facilitate desegregation, the courts redivided the area into eight pie-shaped districts, each of which extended from the central city into the suburbs and beyond to a rural area. The composition of the student population of your district is 35% urban students, 55% suburban students, and 10% rural students. The other seven districts the court created have similar demographic breakdowns. Your district is slightly over 30 miles long and is 15 miles wide at its widest point.

Your school was built in 1976 and was designed to hold 2,500 students. It is the only high school in the district. You have an enrollment of 2,258 and a teaching staff of 146, including 8 special-education teachers and department heads with limited teaching loads. You have 4 assistant principals, an attendance officer, 7 guidance counselors, a full-time athletic director, and the support staff typical of a large school. Your vocational students go to a regional vocational-technical school for their junior and senior years, but you do have a prevocational program in your building.

Your predecessor left to become superintendent in another district, and you assumed the position on July 1. You were new to the district. Two of your assistant principals had applied for the position but were eliminated early in the search. No reason was given for their elimination. Both are looking for principalships elsewhere. One of them is strongly disliked by the staff, and the other was the candidate supported by the teachers.

PROBLEM 27—THE INDUSTRIAL ARTS DEPARTMENT HEAD: A CASE OF INSUBORDINATION

Part 1—A Teacher Flexes His Muscles

Bruno Latham has been head of the industrial arts department and head of vocational education for the past 18 years. He is well liked by his students, and they are fiercely loyal to him. When you begin to inventory incoming supplies during the summer, you notice that the industrial arts supplies have already reached their budgeted amount. You check the purchase orders and discover that only about half of their supplies have come in. It appears that the industrial arts program has spent about twice its budgeted amount, and that your predecessor approved the expenditures. The excess must come out of the supply budgets for the rest of the departments.

You try to reach Mr. Latham on the phone but find he is not home and will not be back until the day before school opens, some two weeks from now. You call the business manager in the central office and find out that she is unaware of any special provision for increasing expenditures for the industrial arts program. She keeps track of your supply expenditures as a whole and feels it is your job to monitor the spending of each department. You call your predecessor and find out that Mr. Latham has been exceeding his budget for years, but never to this extent. The former principal says that Mr. Latham must have taken advantage of the confusion at the end of the year and the fact that a new principal was coming on board to slip extra purchase orders through. Although polite, the tone of your predecessor's voice says that it's your problem now.

Case Questions

1. When you are new to the position, what do you do with a department head who has gotten away with abusing the system for years?
2. What must you find out before proceeding?
3. What alternatives do you have to curb Bruno's spending?

Part 2—The Plot Thickens

On the day before school opens, you finally get to meet Bruno Latham. He says that everyone is well aware that the nature of industrial education is changing rapidly and that the old standard vocational fields–auto repair, electrician training, hairdressing, carpentry, and plumbing–are no longer going to provide students with real job opportunities. Industrial arts must move into robotics, computer-assisted drafting, and laser printing if it is to be of value to students.

You say that he may have a point but that, although you expect him, as department head, to be an advocate of his program and to fight for a fair share of the budget, the ultimate decision is not his to make. You feel you have no choice but to honor the purchase orders approved by your predecessor, since they have already been sent out, but you will not approve another cent for the industrial arts department for this academic year. Mr. Latham must live with what he has.

You remind him that the primary thrust of the vocational program must be at the regional center. It is not possible for any individual school to continually update industrial equipment to keep pace with developments in technology. You point out that many people are still able to make decent, honorable livings as carpenters, electricians, mechanics, plumbers, and beauticians. Those occupations form the base of industrial arts at the secondary level, and to abandon them in favor of a technology that may be obsolete before the students ever get into the job market is folly.

It is not a pleasant confrontation, but you feel the matter is closed, at least for the present.

For a while the problem seems to be settled. At the end of October, however, you receive a bill for acetylene and oxygen and other welding supplies for which no purchase order was ever approved. You call Mr. Latham into your office and demand to know what he means by ordering supplies without approval. He says that in the past he has always had an understanding that, when he needed basic supplies such as these, he could simply order them by phone. You say that you clearly told him that he was not to spend another cent because he was already grossly over budget. He says that the acetylene and the oxygen are necessary to teach the basic skills you are so committed to and that he redesigned his entire program to meet your obsolete ideas of what he should be teaching.

You say that his actions are clearly insubordinate and that you will write an official letter of reprimand for his file. You say that, if there is one more such incident, you will ask the superintendent and the school board to levy a fine in the amount of the over-budget expenditure. You do write such a letter for his file. You also write letters to every supplier Mr. Latham has used in the past five years, saying that they are not to ship any supplies to the school unless they first receive a signed purchase order.

Case Questions

1. Do you think you underreacted at the time of the first confrontation?
2. What other action, if any, might you have taken on the day before the opening of school?
3. In retrospect, might you have reacted better by taking some other course of action at the time of the second confrontation?
4. What do you expect in the future from Mr. Latham?

Part 3—The Tie

Your relationship with Bruno Latham has been strained at best, but he has not done anything overtly insubordinate and has not ordered any more supplies. One of the members of his department is a first-year teacher, Martin Burke, whom you supervise. During your first observation, you note that Mr. Burke is wearing a tie while using machinery. As part of your evaluation, you note that ties are not to be worn when using machinery. In your postobservation conference he acknowledges your comment about the tie and says that he will be sure to remove it in the future when operating a machine.

Two days later you are notified that Martin Burke is filing a grievance against you. The grievance is difficult to understand, but at the heart of it is the statement that, by denying him the right to wear a tie, you are denigrating his position and making him less than a teacher. He states that for a male teacher a tie is a sign of dignity and authority. You recognize that the grievance stems not from Mr. Burke, but rather from Mr. Latham. You deny the grievance and respond to the charges by telling Mr. Burke and his union representative that you never said Mr. Burke couldn't wear a tie in general. You only told him not to wear one when operating or being near machinery. You point out that it is a safety requirement. In fact, it would be a good example to the students if Mr. Burke wore a tie while lecturing and then took it off when operating a machine.

You notify the superintendent because you believe the matter may be taken to the next level, the central office. That is in fact what happens. Once the matter is before the superintendent, Bruno Latham joins the union representative and Martin Burke in testifying that the particular equipment Mr. Burke was operating during your observation was not equipment for which a tie would present a danger. Mr. Latham testifies that your lack of knowledge of industrial arts led you to an incorrect conclusion. In the guise of demonstrating your lack of understanding of his department, Mr. Latham points out that you would not let him purchase acetylene and oxygen and made him change his whole curriculum to an outdated form of instruction.

When the superintendent gets back to you on this matter, you tell him about your past relationship with Mr. Latham. The superintendent says that the man must be put in his place and that, since he has chosen to use his new department member to bring the matter before the superintendent, the central office will deal with the matter. He tells you not to concern yourself with it further and says that he will back you completely. He gives you no idea what action he plans to take now.

Then, two days later, a steady stream of industrial arts students come into the office to give your secretary receipts for film they purchased with their own money for graphic arts projects. They have been told that Mr. Latham said you would reimburse them for their expenditures.

Case Questions

1. Did you handle the observation and evaluation of Martin Burke properly? If not, what might you have done differently?

2. Once the grievance was filed, should you have done anything differently? If so, what?

3. What is the superintendent doing by taking on responsibility for further action in this case?

4. What courses of action are open to the superintendent now?

5. Should you insist on continuing to be involved with the grievance procedure now that it has been moved up to the next level?

6. Martin Burke is a nontenured teacher. How do you plan to deal with him in the future?

7. How do you anticipate the rest of the faculty will respond to this matter?

8. Was there something else you should have done when dealing with Bruno Latham and the acetylene?

9. How do you intend to deal with Mr. Latham in the future?

10. What do you do about the students who expect reimbursement for the film purchases?

SUGGESTED ACTIVITY: Determine what the bases are for dismissal and nonrenewal of a tenured teacher in your state.

PROBLEM 28—THE BOMB SCARE: CRIME AND PUNISHMENT

Part 1—The Evacuation

It is just after 7:00 in the evening. You have just gotten home from school and are beginning supper. You stayed for the beginning of the girl's junior varsity (JV) basketball game at 6:00 and then slipped out to see your family and have a quick meal. You intend to go back to school for the second half of the girls' varsity game. The girls' varsity team is in contention for the league championship.

It is mid-January, it is snowing, and the temperature is 12 degrees, not counting wind chill. There had been talk of rescheduling the game, but the difficulty of finding an open date resulted in a decision to play as scheduled.

The phone rings. It is the superintendent, saying that someone has called in a bomb threat to the athletic director's office. The athletic director has ordered the evacuation of the building. The superintendent tells you to get back to the school as quickly as possible. He'll meet you there.

When you arrive at the school, the visiting team is in its bus with the heat on. Some members of your team are in cars, others are standing in front of the school. All the players are in their uniforms. The JV game was not quite over, so both the JV and the varsity players are suited up. Most of the spectators are in their cars; some have left. You ask the players on the visiting team if those of your players who are not already in cars may join them in the bus. They agree.

The athletic director says that, with 3 minutes left to play in the JV game, she was called out of the gym to take a phone call. She says that a voice sounding like an adolescent boy said that a large pipe bomb had been planted in the building and was set to go off at 7:30. The caller then hung up. She phoned the superintendent, who advised her to evacuate the building immediately, and she did. She has not called the fire department or the police, but she assumes that the superintendent has. You enter the building and call the emergency services number. You find that no one had notified either the police or fire department before your call. Both agencies say they will have people on the scene immediately.

The fire department, the police department, and the superintendent arrive shortly. You tell the fire chief what you know about the bomb threat. He instructs crews to begin searching the building and asks you to find some staff and begin checking lockers. You ask the athletic director and a few teachers, who are standing among the people who have been evacuated, to help you search the lockers. The athletic director says she will do it under protest. Two of the teachers immediately agree, and a third refuses, saying that such a request after normal school hours is inappropriate.

The four of you begin a locker search, using your passkeys. Some of the lockers have nonregulation locks on them. You get cutters from the fire department to remove them. In one locker you find a shotgun and shells. One of your teachers finds several plastic bags containing assorted pills in another locker. He turns them in to you. You turn the shotgun, ammunition, and pills over to the police.

In about a half-hour the fire chief declares that the gym, the locker rooms, and the area immediately around the gym are clear and says that you may allow the people standing outside to reenter the building. When you go out to tell everyone that they may come into the gym area only, you find that the visiting team bus has departed, leaving your players standing outside by the entrance. The assistant coach of the visiting team is there with her van. She has been instructed to wait until the building is cleared and then to collect all her team's clothing and equipment to take them back to her school. She explains that the head coach decided to leave because, with the long delay and the worsening weather, there seemed no sense in staying. The games will have to be rescheduled.

Your players are dangerously cold as they reenter the building.

Case Questions

1. Did you have the right to ask members of your staff to search lockers? If anything had happened to them during the search, would you have been personally liable?

2. Was the teacher who refused to search acting within his rights, or is this a case of insubordination?

3. When searching the lockers for a pipe bomb, do you have the right to seize drugs and weapons? May you turn them over to the police? Can they then be used as evidence in court?

4. Did you provide prudently for the welfare of your basketball players?

5. In this case everyone assumed that someone else had notified the police and fire departments. Are you liable for any damages caused by the delay? Is the athletic director? The superintendent?

Part 2—The Aftermath

Once everyone is back in the building, you leave the search of the remainder of the school to the fire department and your staff. You ask if anyone saw anything suspicious or has anything to report in this matter. Most of the spectators have gone home, as have many of the players. You ask that anyone who has anything to report tell you then or within the next day. No one comes forward. The remaining members of the girls' team change out of their uniforms and leave. The assistant coach of the visiting team collects all the clothing and belongings and leaves. The search teams find nothing, and by 8:30 the chief has declared the building clear. Everyone leaves.

The next morning two members of the girls' varsity team report that they have suffered frostbite in their toes. Several of the players who left right after the visiting team departed report that many of their valuables are missing. You receive a call from the principal of the school your students were playing. He says that he would like your district to reimburse his team for the bus used to transport his players to your building and for several items that were not recovered from the locker room by the assistant coach. You say that you were astounded that his head coach just ordered your players out of their bus without considering what might happen to them in the cold and snow.

Case Questions

1. Is your district responsible for the missing valuables?
2. Who must bear responsibility for the girls who were frostbitten?
3. Should you reimburse the visiting team for their expenses?
4. Is there anything else you might do to further the investigation at this point?

Part 3—The Culprits

At the time of the incident, you and the superintendent talked with several people you thought might know something about who made the phone call. You got some leads, and you follow them up the next day by compiling lists of those present at various places and times. Eventually you start to hear about a small, timid freshman named Dale, who may have been in the main entrance hall right outside the gym at the time the bomb scare was phoned in.

You call Dale to your office and, after some questioning, discover that he thinks he overheard Jon Stebbins and Roger South plotting to make the call from the pay phone in the lobby. Jon and Roger are two disaffected students who currently hold the record for the largest number of detentions and out-of-school suspensions. You know Jon and Roger to be bullies, and you can understand why Dale has been reluctant to come forward. You promise that you will not reveal the source of your information, and Dale confides that he did hear the two boys plotting the call but that they left the hall where he was standing and went into the lobby, where the pay phone was. He did not actually hear the call itself.

Dale is worried, because he had told only his best friend and he feels that his friend must have spread the story until it got to you. He is afraid of being beaten up by Jon and Roger and says that he wants to be kept out of it. You promise him that you will not give them his name.

You call Jon and Roger to your office and say that you have evidence that they phoned in the bomb scare. You tell them that what they have done is a felony and that the matter must be turned over to the police. You ask if they have anything to say in their defense. They both deny having anything to do with the bomb scare and will admit only that they were at the game. They claim that they left the game to go outside to have a cigarette and were in fact outside smoking when everyone was being evacuated from the building. They claim that you are just picking on them because you need someone to take the blame and you hate them because of their past records. They demand that you prove it was them. You say they are facing expulsion and arrest if they do not cooperate. They demand that you produce evidence.

Case Questions

1. Do you believe you now know who made the call?
2. How do you proceed from here?
3. What type of evidence must you produce in order to have the school board expel Jon and Roger?
4. Is it time to turn the matter over to the police? If not, what must you do first?
5. What moral, ethical, and legal obligations do you have to protect Dale? How can it be done?
6. Are there any circumstances under which you could hold Jon and Roger and their families responsible for payment of damages caused by the bomb scare?
7. How might you have handled this matter better?
8. What policy or practice regarding bomb scares might be established to ensure the safety of students, staff, and your building in the future?

SUGGESTED ACTIVITY: Find out the law in your state regarding search and seizure of illegal substances by school officials and the use of such evidence in court.

PROBLEM 29—THE ALCOHOLIC TEACHER: BECOMING INVOLVED IN THE PERSONAL LIFE OF A FACULTY MEMBER

Part 1—The Drunk

Since this is your first year in a large school, you have decided to do all the teacher observations and staff evaluations yourself. Your assistants can do the second and third observations of nontenured staff as needed. You have found the range of teachers you anticipated in a school this size. Some deserve commendation and some need substantial improvement. Until you got to Joanne Miller, however, you had found no teacher functioning at such a low level that you felt obliged to consider removing that teacher from his or her position in midcontract.

Joanne Miller is in her 19th year as an English teacher in your building. She is a Princeton graduate who wrote two fairly successful novels many years ago. She has an MA in English from Brown, where she was a graduate teaching fellow, and an MS in education from the University of New York at Albany. From her personnel record you note that she is 54. She looks at least 15 years older. Her clothing is worn and soiled, and she has an offensive body odor. She appeared to be drunk when you observed her teaching. Her instruction was incoherent, and she had very poor classroom control even though the class you observed was a junior honors section.

Before you commit anything to paper, you call your superintendent and report what you have observed. He tells you that everyone in the system knows about Joanne, and most feel sorry for her. She used to be a very dynamic teacher and a great writer, but all that is long gone. She needs to finish out this year and work one more before she can collect a pension. The plan is to tolerate her until that time and then force her to take early retirement.

You contemplate what you should do. The path of least resistance is to go along with the superintendent's plan and endure Joanne for another year and a half. You have two other concerns, however. First, how can you induce other weak teachers to improve when no one else appears to be performing nearly as poorly as Joanne Miller? Second, what message are you giving the students about substance abuse if you are willing to accept it in a teacher?

Earlier you had become acquainted with Bruce Eaton. Bruce is a member of the economics department, the vice president of the teachers' union, and the head of the substance abuse prevention task force. He is an acknowledged recovering alcoholic. He is free third period, and you ask to see him in your office. When he comes in, you say that you have a serious concern about a member of the faculty whom you believe to be an alcoholic. He replies that there are at least seven active alcoholics on the faculty but the obvious one is Joanne Miller. He says she is in the last stages of the disease. You ask if he has any advice as to what you might do to help her. You tell him you are not willing to tolerate her behavior. He asks how serious you are, and you respond that you are very serious.

Bruce tells you that he has been sober for four years and has been a member of Alcoholics Anonymous for all that time. He says that even at his worst, which was pretty bad, he had never progressed as far in the disease as Joanne. He asks if you are willing to try a drastic measure. He does not believe that anything short of it will help at this stage. You ask what it is, and he says that it is something called a confrontation. He explains that you must gather all the people who are close to Joanne and have them tell her to her face how her drinking has affected them and what they want her to do about it. You must go last and say that her teaching is so poor that, if she does not seek treatment immediately, you will begin collecting data to present to the school board to have her fired for incompetence.

Bruce says that a confrontation must be well planned and well executed. He has participated in some but is not expert enough to conduct one. If you are interested, he can put you in touch with someone associated with a regional hospital's treatment program, who can help arrange what is needed. He suggests you think about it and, if you are willing to commit yourself to such a step, see him tomorrow third period.

Case Questions

1. You are contemplating taking a step that will involve you deeply and intimately in a subordinate's life. Do you have the ethical and moral right to take such a step?

2. You are not personally familiar with the procedure Bruce is advising. Do you trust him to arrange something as potentially dramatic as what he proposes?

3. How can you find out more about confrontations and their effectiveness?

4. Your superintendent has said that the plan is to allow Joanne Miller to complete her 20 years and then get rid of her. Will you be putting your job in jeop-

ardy if you try another course? What reaction are you likely to get from the central office and the rest of the faculty?

5. What outcome is likely if Joanne refuses to enter treatment after the confrontation?

Part 2—The Confrontation

The next day, during third period, you speak to Bruce. You have decided that you need to know more about the possible results of a confrontation before making any decision. Bruce says frankly that he had never thought you would seriously consider the confrontation option but that, since meeting with you yesterday, he has spoken with several people about the situation.

He tells you that the regional medical facility anticipates that a bed in its 30-day treatment program will open up in 18 days. If you can plan the confrontation for that date, you can get Joanne into detoxification and the 30-day program immediately after the confrontation. Doing that will give her the greatest possible chance for success. Furthermore, Bruce has checked with the district's medical insurance plan and found that Joanne will be fully covered. She has a high rate of absenteeism, however, and has very few sick days and no personal leave days left. Bruce proposes using union benefit funds, if necessary, to pay her rent and utilities while she is in treatment.

Bruce goes on to explain that he has identified several people who are important to Joanne. She has no family, but she did raise a foster son, and there are some neighbors and several teachers who are or were close to her. Bruce has spoken with most of them, and everyone he contacted is willing to try to convince Joanne that she has a disease and must get treatment for it.

He proposes getting six substitutes to cover various classes on the day of the confrontation and offers to have his car filled with gas and ready to take Joanne to the medical center immediately afterward if she agrees. He wants another teacher who is also in AA to go with them.

Bruce says that you will have the most important role. He reiterates that you must be prepared to point out what a poor teacher Joanne has become, that you attribute her poor performance to her drinking, and that if she refuses to enter treatment you will move immediately to have her dismissed on the grounds of incompetence. You are also to say that, if she does enter the program, you are prepared to give her as much support as possible when she returns. You must stand by what you say.

Bruce goes on to say that, if you agree to attempt this confrontation, you should be prepared for the shock waves it will send throughout the school. He also warns that the confrontation must be kept secret from Joanne. You are to ask to see her for a minute, get her into the conference room, have her sit down among all the people closest to her, and begin the confrontation before she has time to put up all her defenses.

You call the director of a substance abuse program you have heard others commend. You describe the situation to her without disclosing any names. She says that the information you have heard is correct and that a confrontation is by far the best hope for saving your teacher's life. From the symptoms you have described, the director estimates that your teacher is very near the end of her life unless the deterioration is halted immediately. She asks who has given you your information and who would conduct the confrontation. You give her Bruce's name. She says that she cannot admit to knowing other members of AA but that you should feel confident that things will be done the right way with the resources you have. She warns you that sometimes confrontations do not work or do not work the first time, and she says you must be prepared to do what you say you will do. If the confrontation does not work, you must not blame yourself.

Case Questions

1. Bruce has done a great deal more in the past 24 hours than you expected. How do you feel about that?
2. If you decide to go ahead with the confrontation, will you take charge or simply back up Bruce's efforts?
3. Do you think Bruce is right about there being extensive repercussions if you go ahead with his plan?
4. If you decide to try the confrontation, how will you inform the superintendent? What will you do if the superintendent says that you must accept full responsibility for the outcome of this measure if you go ahead?
5. If you choose not to have the confrontation, what signals will you be sending to the students, the faculty, and the teachers' union? What will happen to your relationship with Bruce?
6. What might the repercussions be if you do proceed? What might this action do at a time when the faculty is still forming its impressions of you?
7. Will you go ahead with the confrontation?
8. How will you feel about yourself if you do not have the confrontation?

SUGGESTED ACTIVITY: Investigate the services available for substance abusers of all ages in your area.

PROBLEM 30—THE STAGED FIGHT: APPLYING THE RULES

Tom and Ted Franklin are 16-year-old twins who come from the rural part of your school district. They are big, solid kids, the kind you can depend on to clean up after a dance or build sets for the school plays. They are good natured, but only mediocre academically. They are also avid hunters, and tomorrow is the first day of hunting season. You have been told that a very high percentage of the boys from the rural part of the county will be sick tomorrow. The staff calls it "buck fever," and past practice has been to give the boys an excused absence if their parents write a note saying they were sick. Your alternative is to comb the woods.

Right at lunchtime you hear a commotion immediately outside your office. You go out and see Tom and Ted punching each other and cursing each other very loudly. You tell them to stop it, and they do immediately. Since all the punches were going wide of their mark, it is obvious to you that the two boys staged the fight for the purpose of getting the standard punishment for fighting: out-of-school suspension.

If you follow standard procedure and suspend the twins, you will be doing exactly what they want you to do. You feel the perfect solution would be an in-school suspension. The policy set by the school board, however, is very specific on the penalty for fighting. There was an in-school suspension policy several years ago, but it was discontinued. You have been trying unsuccessfully to reestablish it.

It is tempting just to suspend Tom and Ted and let them go hunting. There are, after all, many much more serious matters to consider. What you have noticed, however, is a schoolwide attitude toward discipline in which many offenses are overlooked, especially if they are committed by likable students. For years senior, junior, and even sophomore skip days have been ignored. Despite a strict no-smoking policy, everyone knows that the area in the back of the cafeteria near the dumpsters is used by students who smoke. The unwritten rule is that, as long as students confine their smoking to that area, no one will say anything. Students are almost never reported late for class, even though the halls are crowded for nearly a minute after the late bell rings.

You have asked your assistant principals and several teachers about discipline in the school, and they have all said that it is impossible to enforce every rule. If they don't close their eyes to some of the petty offenses and concentrate on keeping a lid on the more serious problems, the school will become like a police state and will eventually really explode. Your job description clearly says that the primary responsibility for discipline lies with the classroom teachers and the assistant principals. You are to be the first line of appeal in the more serious cases.

Case Questions

1. What do you think of the staff's attitude toward discipline?
2. Do you feel that overlooking certain transgressions affects the school climate? If so, in what way?
3. As a new principal, should you take action to enforce a policy if ignoring the policy has long been standard practice? Would it be wiser to wait until you are more fully established? Is the best way to establish yourself to take firm action against past practices?
4. Are you comfortable with the standards described in this problem?
5. If you choose to tighten discipline in this instance, how will you go about it?
6. If the staff, the central office, and the school board are all satisfied with the present discipline standards, is it wise to try to enforce neglected rules? Is it even *possible* to enforce them?
7. Should a new principal be an agent for change? Do you make changes primarily to bring the school closer to your personal vision of what a school should be?

8. What will you do with Tom and Ted?

SUGGESTED ACTIVITY: Write a description of the way you would choose to review a discipline policy.

PROBLEM 31—THE LESBIAN COUPLE: DEFUSING SITUATIONS

Margo Stedman is a student in charge of selling tickets to the junior prom. Because of past problems with students attending the prom stag, for several years tickets have been sold only to couples. Margo has asked to see you because Judy Markham and Patty Cooper, both juniors, insist that they be sold tickets to the junior prom as a couple. They have declared that they are lesbian lovers. Tickets to the junior prom have always been sold only to heterogeneous couples.

Margo says that everyone has known about Judy and Patty for a long time and no one has ever bothered them. She believes that the two girls are trying to start some sort of crusade. She has heard that the courts ordered a school somewhere else to allow a male gay couple to attend a prom, and she imagines that she will have no choice but to sell them the tickets. What she wants is to keep the prom from becoming a circus. She doesn't personally care what sort of relationship Judy and Patty have or even whether they come to the prom together. What she wants is to make sure that their coming doesn't ruin the event for everyone else. She wants you to speak to the two girls and make sure that their intention is only to attend the prom like anyone else and not to turn it into a platform for espousing their life-style.

Case Questions

1. Do you believe that gay and lesbian couples should be allowed to attend formal school-sponsored dances together?
2. Do you believe that the courts would force you to allow Judy and Patty to attend as a couple if you attempted to exclude them?
3. If Judy and Patty are going to attend the prom, is there any way you can minimize the impact of their presence?
4. Do you think outside advocacy groups are likely to descend on your school if Judy and Patty attend? If they are prevented from attending? If so, what preparations can you make for dealing with such groups?
5. Do you believe that the news media are likely to inflate the attendance of a lesbian couple at the prom into more than it is?
6. Are you likely to accomplish anything by talking to the girls? What approach would you take with them?
7. What do you tell Margo, who is sitting in your office waiting for your response?
8. At what point do you notify the central office of the girls' decision?

9. Do you believe that Judy and Patty's determination to attend the prom will infringe on the rights of the other students to have the sort of junior prom experience they want?

10. Is this still a burning social issue, or has it begun to lose its potency through repetition?

SUGGESTED ACTIVITY: Determine how you would respond if a television reporter and a camera crew requested an interview or suddenly started taping in front of your school.

PROBLEM 32—JAMIE'S SUICIDE: DEALING WITH GRIEF AND ANGER

Part 1—The Initial Shock

Jamie Malloy was a 16-year-old boy whose mother had died the year before, after a prolonged struggle with cancer. His father is a teacher in the middle school where his 13-year-old sister is a student. Jamie was a studious, withdrawn boy who got straight A's without effort. He was not athletic, and although he had his own circle of friends among his fellow juniors, he was not generally popular.

In October he learned that his father had cancer. His father began treatment, the same sort of treatment his mother had undergone. Jamie told his guidance counselor he didn't know if he could go through seeing another parent die a slow and painful death. The doctors gave his father a 50% chance of survival.

Jamie was absent from school on the Friday before Thanksgiving. Saturday morning his body was found in his car. He had driven to a secluded spot, diverted the car exhaust into the driver's window, and asphyxiated himself. Word of Jamie's death spread quickly. The prayer service at Jamie's church Sunday night was given over to the junior class. The church was filled beyond capacity.

On Sunday night you called your department heads and asked them to call the members of their departments to inform them that there would be a meeting at 7:00 Monday morning in the auditorium to discuss how to handle the suicide. You arrange for trained counselors to be present to assist in preparing the teachers to respond to what they might encounter and to help some of the faculty members work through their own grief and anger. You are especially concerned about the faculty because the victim was the son of a colleague. More than 90% of the faculty came to the meeting, despite the short notice. According to contract, all faculty meetings must be announced at least 1 week in advance.

You could tell just by watching the first students arrive that today would not be a typical day. The last teen suicide had occurred 2 years ago and in July. More recently two teen deaths had been questionable. One was a drug overdose, and in the other a car had smashed into a tree. This one was different.

At the beginning of third period, the president of the junior class asks to have all juniors called into the cafeteria for a brief meeting and asks you to be present. From what you have seen, the other students have settled into the usual routine, but the junior class has not. You authorize the impromptu meeting.

You are the only adult present at the meeting. The assembled juniors exhibit a mixture of reactions. Several girls are crying. There is a knot of boys, mostly the urban and tougher suburban part of the population, who are making crude jokes. Jamie had belonged to the suburban contingent. Some juniors are angry, others remote, and some bored.

Even before all the members of the class have arrived, a heated debate breaks out between, on one hand, those who feel Jamie committed a cowardly sin that can only inflict intense pain on his father and sister and, on the other hand, those who feel that he had a right to end his life if he found it unbearable. A few say that his death was no great loss, and they are angry that everyone is making so much of it.

You let the students express themselves freely for a time. After a few minutes, you say that the meeting was called at the request of the junior class president, and you ask everyone to be quiet so that he can address them.

The president says that some of the people gathered here liked Jamie, some did not, and others didn't really know him. He says that everyone, even those making crude jokes about suicide, has been affected by the news. He goes on to say that first they owe Jamie a minute of silence. The group becomes absolutely still, even those students who had been joking.

At the end of the minute the student leader asks how many people went to the prayer meeting at the church last night. About a third of the students raise their hands. He asks how many feel angry at Jamie, and again about a third raise their hands. How many really consider themselves Jamie's friend? About a quarter of the students raise their hands. The class president says that a lot of the people who just raised their hands wouldn't have wanted Jamie to sit at their table at lunch, let alone have done things with him outside of school.

He asks how many people suspected that Jamie might commit suicide. About two dozen students raise their hands. He asks how many students have thought about committing suicide. A few students raise their hands. He tells the students to be honest, and he raises his own hand. About half the students raise their hands. He says, "I don't believe the rest of you." The vast majority of the remaining students raise their hands. He says that now they are being truthful. He says that only a few students present were really close to Jamie. Many of Jamie's real friends didn't come to school today.

The president turns to you and says there are three things he wants to ask in the name of the junior class. First, he wants the school to lower its flag to half-mast. Second, he wants all members of the junior class who wish to go to the funeral tomorrow to be able to go without penalty. Third, he wants the school to form and sponsor a teen suicide prevention hotline.

Case Questions

1. If you had been specifically invited to the Sunday night prayer service at Jamie's church, would you have gone?

2. Do you think you overreacted by having the 7:00 a.m. meeting? Did it make sense to bring in outside counselors?

3. Did you do the right thing by allowing the junior class president to call a meeting of his class in the middle of the school day?

4. Would you have anticipated that Jamie's suicide would cause much disruption in a school of this size? There are more than 500 students in the junior class.

5. What would you have done if the junior class president had asked the students to pray instead of having a minute of silence?

6. What do you think of the way the junior class president handled himself? What is your opinion of what he said?

7. How will you respond to his three requests?

8. Should you have been the only adult present?

Part 2—The Rest of the Day

The impromptu junior class meeting has taken about 25 minutes. You dismiss the students, telling them to go back to class. You go back to your office and make an announcement over the public address system, saying that all juniors should be reporting to their classes shortly. By the beginning of the next period, you have discovered that several juniors never returned to class after the meeting. You make another announcement over the PA, saying that you want all teachers to take attendance and send reports on it to the office, just as they would at the beginning of the school day. When the reports are complete, you find that 54 students who were in school are no longer in class. The nurse can account for 7 students, who were sent home, leaving 47 unaccounted for, almost all of them juniors. You have your secretaries begin calling the parents of the 47, informing them that their children have left the building without permission. You get into your car and take a quick swing through a nearby miniplaza. You find 9 students there and order them all back to school. You give them the usual penalty for skipping school, and are secretly glad that all 9 of them return as you instructed.

Meanwhile, some of the parents have called, saying their children have come home because they are upset about Jamie. The parents indicate that, under the circumstances, they are giving their children permission to stay home. Many of the calls went to the guidance counselors because you were out tracking down students. The head of guidance said, that because of the unusual circumstances, any child who had decided to go home would not be penalized. There are still 26 students unaccounted for.

Case Questions

1. Should you have anticipated that many students would leave the building after the meeting?

2. Was it wise to drive to the miniplaza to find students? What would you have done if they had refused to return to school? Did you have any legal authority over the students once they left school grounds?

3. You have punished the students who were at the miniplaza. What about the ones the guidance counselor pardoned? How do you respond to the head of guidance for issuing amnesty?

4. What do you do about the students whose parents have now given them permission to stay home for the remainder of the day?

5. Are you and the district liable for any injury that might befall those students who left the building?

6. Should you have left the discipline matter to your assistant principals, as you would normally? Was it reasonable for you to become so involved in matters normally outside your realm of functioning? Did you need to keep a high profile in this case?

SUGGESTED ACTIVITY: Delineate the advantages and disadvantages of adopting a direct, personal, high-profile approach to leadership in a large high school.

PROBLEM 33—CHEERLEADERS: EQUAL OPPORTUNITY

Part 1—Males Invade Female Turf

Before you became principal, the district had undergone a series of challenges from feminist groups concerning Title IX violations in the sports program. For fall sports you now have boys' and girls' cross-country, girls' touch football (which replaced field hockey), boys' football (still an all-male sport), and girls' and boys' soccer teams. In winter you have boys' and girls' varsity and junior varsity basketball and girls' and boys' volleyball. The district dropped hockey and wrestling because it could not have coed teams in those sports and there were no female equivalents. Volleyball was an addition. There are coed swimming and ski teams. In the spring the school has girls' softball, boys' baseball, and coed golf, tennis, and track.

There is still much dissatisfaction among male athletes at having to give up wrestling and hockey, but you have been told that all Title IX regulations have been satisfied and the issues have all been resolved.

Yesterday was the first day of practice for cheerleaders, and nine boys, all former hockey players and wrestlers, showed up and demanded that they be allowed to try out. Rhonda Hirsh, the cheerleading coach and one of the female physical education teachers, has come into your office and says that she will not tolerate boys on the squad. She says that the boys are there only to protest their sports' having been cut. She was one of the people who thought that the wrestling and hockey programs should have been allowed to continue even without female athletes. Several years ago she was the girls' field hockey coach, and she also fought to preserve that program. She says that cheerleading is being compromised because of stupid concessions that were made to pressure groups. Your response is that many high schools now have coed cheerleading squads, and that the males are used for lifts. Rhonda says that she would consider a coed squad if she thought the boys were there because of a genuine interest in cheerleading. The boys who showed up were there for purposes of protest and were entirely negative in their attitude.

You tell her you understand that the conflict over the sports program was long and bitter and that new controversy will only reopen old wounds. You advise that she hold auditions as announced, evaluate each candidate on merit, and get on with coaching her squad. You say that the protesters will fade away if they are truly not interested in cheering. She is not pleased with your response, but she leaves.

What you have left unsaid is that you have already received numerous protests from the parents of white athletes who say that there are disproportional numbers of black students on the football and basketball teams and that the black athletes try to force out the remaining white athletes. There has already been at least one serious racially motivated fight between black and white football players in the locker room. Your assessment of Rhonda's concern is that the outcome is a foregone conclusion. You will simply have a coed cheering squad, and she should have realized that by now, with everything that has gone on in the recent past.

Case Questions

1. Do you think the school should have given up the field hockey, wrestling, and hockey programs? Could you have offered another solution that would meet the Title IX regulations?

2. What, if anything, do you intend to do about the parents' complaints about racial imbalance on teams?

3. What can you do to minimize racial tension on your sports teams?

4. Do you feel there is any need to follow up with Rhonda Hirsh? If so, how?

Part 2—Uniforms

Long ago Rhonda Hirsh had developed a series of tests to determine who would be on the cheerleading squad. She had developed the tests to eliminate charges of favoritism in selecting cheerleaders. She now uses the tests to deal with the boys who have come out for the squad. Two of the nine boys drop out quickly. Four of the remaining seven are unable to do the gymnastics required and thus are eliminated by the tests. Three of the boys make the final cut, including John Spitzer, who meets all the standards for the varsity squad. If there is one boy Rhonda hoped to eliminate, it is John. She has had him in physical education and thinks of him as a real wise guy.

Now that the final cuts have been made, it is time to issue uniforms, and she does. The new cheerleading uniforms are much less conservative than the old ones. All the uniforms are clearly designed for female cheerleaders. She hands them out and says that all students who wish to be cheerleaders must wear the selected uniforms. The two boys on the junior varsity squad angrily throw down the uniforms and leave. John suits up. When he comes back out into the gym, the girls break into gales of laughter. John curtsies. He says that, the way the uniform is cut, the first time he does a jump he'll make himself instantly popular with all the women in attendance. The remarks become more ribald from there. Rhonda says that is quite enough and that he is being eliminated from the team for being disruptive and disrespectful.

While John is performing in the gym, the other two boys are in your office. They complain bitterly about the way they were treated. They say there is no way they can wear the uniforms. One of the two, Ray Sanchez, says that he might have had a chance for a wrestling scholarship to college if the team hadn't been disbanded. His family thought about suing the school to force it to reestablish the team. There were other wrestlers and hockey players who considered the same sort of action. Only the intervention of the former principal kept them from taking the matter to court. Today's insult is the last straw. Ray will see to it that wrestling and hockey are restored. He storms out of your office.

Just as Ray is leaving, John appears. He is the quintessential clown, and between his antics and his appearance, you cannot help laughing. You tell John and the other boy that you will take care of the matter. John is to go back to the gym immediately and change, and both boys are to report to you before the start of classes in the morning.

You immediately go to the gym and ask to speak to Rhonda Hirsh privately. You ask how she could have done such a thing, knowing the history of the situation. You tell her to rush-order cheerleading uniforms appropriate for males. She says that the budget for uniforms has been completely expended. You say you will find the necessary funds, and you give her a purchase order number and form. You order her to reinstate the three boys immediately, to select appropriate uniforms from one of her catalogs, and to phone the order in this afternoon.

Case Questions

1. Do high school athletes have a reasonable case to bring to court if a sport they have participated in is dropped? What about the loss of college scholarship possibilities?
2. How are you going to deal with Ray Sanchez?
3. What further steps do you plan to take with Rhonda Hirsh?
4. Should John Spitzer be punished for his ribald remarks and antics?
5. Can you do anything to prevent the carefully worked-out compromise on athletics from falling apart?
6. Is it time to involve the central office?
7. Do you need to find out more about what really happened regarding the sports program before you were hired? If so, how do you go about it?

Part 3—The New Uniforms

Eight days have passed and the new uniforms have arrived. Suddenly virtually all the female cheerleaders are demanding to see you. It seems Rhonda Hirsh ordered loose-fitting sweat-suit-style uniforms for all the cheerleaders, not just the boys. Most of the girls are furious, except Carolyn Richardson, who says it's about time the cheerleaders had nonsexist, comfortable uniforms that will keep them warm at football games and in the cold gym.

Case Questions

1. Are typical female cheerleader uniforms sexually exploitative?
2. What immediate steps will you take to settle the uniform matter?
3. How will you deal with Rhonda Hirsh?
4. You had anticipated an expenditure for 3 uniforms. You are now faced with a bill for 35 uniforms. How will you pay it?

SUGGESTED ACTIVITY: Write a position paper describing the extent to which a principal can and should determine the issues the school will focus upon.

PROBLEM 34—THE GOLFER: FORCING A CAREER CHOICE

Part 1—An Ineffectual Teacher

Tom Bannor is a tenured English teacher in his mid-30s. When you observed his teaching, you saw a mediocre performance by a teacher with a cavalier attitude. You pointed out the shortcomings and suggested several ways he could improve.

At basketball games, you have heard casual remarks that Tom uses videotapes extensively. You check the sign-out sheet for the VCR in the English department office, and you note that Tom signs the machine out far more than any other teacher. You then check the media center VCR sign-out sheet and find that Tom accounts for nearly 80% of the use of that machine. You look through the lesson plans he has submitted and do not see any reference to video-oriented lessons.

You casually ask some of Tom's students how he covers the works of literature in his lesson plans. The students tell you that they have seen virtually all of them on tape, that Tom usually introduces an author, often shows a video about the writer's life, talks a bit about the work, and then shows the tape of the work. He sometimes leaves the room for an extended time while a tape is running.

You confront Tom with what you have uncovered. He claims that, although he signs up for the VCR often, he does not use it all that much. He says that he uses videotapes to give the students a feeling for a historical period or to preview Shakespeare because Shakespeare should be seen before it is read. He says that the use of videotapes is a perfectly legitimate element of instruction and that his subject matter happens to lend itself well to that medium. He says he signs up for the VCR just so that one will be available if it seems educationally appropriate to use it. You say that weak teachers often use videotapes to avoid preparing their own lessons and that, to shelter him from such suspicions, you are ordering him to refrain from using video for the remainder of the year. He objects and threatens to file a grievance.

A few days later one of the union representatives asks to speak with you. She says that Tom has asked her to represent him in his grievance against your moratorium on his video use. She says she wants you to understand that as a union official she must follow through on Tom's request but that in this case she does so with reluctance. You hear the grievance and find it without merit. Tom presses on with it, taking it to the superintendent.

In the midst of the grievance process, one of Tom's colleagues in the English department asks to speak with you privately. He tells you that you are taking the wrong approach with Tom. Instead of going after his abuse of videotapes, you should look at the Mondays and Fridays he has called in sick on dates when golf tournaments were held in the state. He says that Tom hates teaching and is hoping to become a golf pro. Tom has been playing the tournament circuit for years, always leaving a videotape for his substitute. The teacher asks you not to let anyone know that he came to speak to you about this matter.

Case Questions

1. What do you think of teachers who use videotapes extensively?
2. Were you on solid ground when you ordered Tom to stop using videotapes?
3. Can you win this grievance? What tactics will you use, now that the matter has been appealed?
4. How can you find out whether Tom has entered golf tournaments on days when he called in sick?
5. What can you tell from the reactions of the union representative and Tom's department colleague?
6. Are you comfortable getting negative information from one teacher about another? Is it unethical for the teacher to give you such information? How do you feel about the teacher's request that his visit remain confidential? Do you want to encourage such behavior?

Part 2—The Option

With the help of some outside resources, you find that Tom not only has played in several tournaments on days when he called in sick, but also has done quite well in them. Now that you know what to look for, you are able to find newspaper accounts of tournaments that mention Tom's name and describe his performance. With that new evidence, you again confront Tom, saying that his abuse of sick days is a clear violation of contract and that, if he does not resign, you will begin the process of having him fired. You are giving him 24 hours to decide.

Case Questions

1. Do you have ample grounds for terminating Tom's contract? For refusing to renew it?
2. Would it have been better to make an example of Tom and go through with the termination procedures rather than allow him to resign? Why or why not?

3. Does the unresolved grievance in the other matter have any bearing on the issue of misuse of sick days? If so, what?

4. How do you choose to work with the central office in this matter?

5. Do you think it will matter to the rest of the staff whether Tom resigns or you dismiss him?

6. What will the staff think if Tom suddenly resigns to pursue a golfing career?

SUGGESTED ACTIVITY: Tom has agreed to resign, but only if you will give him a letter of recommendation for his placement file. If you feel willing to write such a letter, your activity is to write it. If you are not willing to write such a letter, your activity is to describe, in writing, how you will handle the situation from this point onward.

PROBLEM 35—THE DYING DEPARTMENTS: A CASE OF REVISION OR POSSIBLE ELIMINATION

You have been considering staffing needs for next year. Two areas immediately stand out as having very low enrollment: art and home economics. You reach behind you and get the yearbook from 12 years ago. There you find that the art department had $3\frac{3}{5}$ teachers and home economics had 4 teachers. This year the art department has $1\frac{3}{5}$ teachers, and home economics has $1\frac{2}{5}$.

The full-time art teacher has complained that ceramics had to be dropped because new state regulations made it virtually impossible to use the kiln. You look in your files and find that even 12 years ago a ceramics course was offered in the fall and pottery in the spring, one section of each. It may be that the general art courses had a ceramics or pottery component, but only a small part of the decline can be attributed to the loss of the kiln.

Two years ago the state increased the number of credits required in math and social studies, and that may have reduced the numbers of students who could take electives. The school board also broadened the definition of fine arts, so students can now choose from a greater variety of classes to meet that graduation requirement. You are also aware that the feminist movement has had a negative effect on enrollment in home economics classes across the nation. The recent inclusion of a culinary arts program at the regional vocational school has also had a negative effect on the department's enrollment.

What you have now are home economics classes with an average enrollment of nine and art classes with an average enrollment of eight. You cannot justify the expense of maintaining programs with such low enrollment when so many other programs are making increased demands. Also, the supply budgets for the home economics and art departments are very high, as are the equipment replacement costs.

You wonder whether to reduce the offerings in both areas and, if so, how. One of your main concerns is that the skills in each area are too broad for one teacher to do a good job of teaching all the courses in the department. The part-time art position is currently held by someone who also teaches graphics for the industrial arts department. The part-time home economics teacher is a semiretired teacher who prefers to work only in the morning. Your full-time art teacher is certified to teach social studies as well, but your full-time home economics teacher has no other endorsements.

In your observation of the art and home economics teachers, you found that the person whose position is split between art and industrial arts has been steadily increasing the industrial arts part of her assignment. Even the courses she teaches in the art department are associated more closely with the technical and commercial aspects of art than with the creative and traditional. The full-time teacher, Saul Golden, seems much more interested in preparing for showings than in instructing students. He runs a loose program in which students work on their own projects at their own pace. There does not seem to be much teacher–student interaction. The exact opposite was true when you observed the home economics teachers.

In addition, the home economics teachers have always offered to provide refreshments and decorations for school functions. Saul has only reluctantly met your requests that he provide rotating displays of student art in the main lobby, the office, and the media center and maintain displays for two glass-enclosed cases near his room. He claims that such requests are beyond his job description. He has refused to help in any way with the scenery for the school musical and dramatic productions.

Past experience has taught you that teachers in nonacademic areas often provide unique services by way of their special relationships with students who need support and encouragement and don't find it elsewhere. That seems to be happening in the home economics department, but only the best of the art students, those who plan to go on to art school or whose work is entered in outside shows, seem to get any attention from Saul.

Case Questions

1. It is almost time for registration for next year's classes. Both the art department and the home economics department are in danger of losing their part-time staff unless enrollment improves. How will you deal with each department regarding this matter?

2. What do you see as the purpose of having art and home economics programs in a high school? Should such programs be allowed to wither?

3. When Saul was first hired, he was required to teach one social studies class. He did, but not with enthusiasm. He was very glad when he was able to have an assignment entirely in the art department. If you have to reduce the staff in the art department to one full-time teacher, will you have two part-time people or one full-time person? Will you make the same decision about the home economics department?

4. Is it reasonable and appropriate to expect art teachers to provide materials or services to other departments and programs within the school? Is it reasonable and appropriate to expect it of home economics teachers?

5. Should art teachers be expected to maintain displays of student work in the school and perhaps in the central office and public buildings? Is it an abuse of the art faculty, since other teachers are not expected to do such things?

6. Should the home economics department be expected to provide refreshments for such functions as PTA and Booster Club meetings? If so, whose budget should the supplies come from?

7. How do you choose to work with Saul if you think his attitude is poor and his instruction loose? What difference does it make whether Saul is tenured or nontenured?

8. Will you approach the home economics teachers any differently? If so, how?

9. To what extent will you involve each department in deciding what courses to offer next year? In deciding the long-range future of its programs?

10. What can each department do to reverse the decline in its enrollment?

11. Should several small departments be combined into one collective department for administrative purposes, or are they too diverse for a collective approach?

12. Should some traditional departments be phased out? If so, under what circumstances?

SUGGESTED ACTIVITY: Describe how you would acquire an understanding of the content and value of a subject area outside your area of personal expertise.

PROBLEM 36—THE CHEMICAL STORAGE ROOM: MEETING SAFETY STANDARDS

Emmit Mulvaney has been the head of the science department for several years. You find him to be intelligent, cooperative, and pleasant. You make it a point to spend some time with each of your department chairs on a regular basis. Today, in your daily after-school swing through the building, you decide to see what is happening in the science department. Emmit is not in the science department office area or in his classroom. You find him in the science storage room, where he is taking inventory.

This is one of the few places in the school you have not been before. There is a very strong mixture of acrid and noxious odors. You note that there are cans so corroded that anything that may have been written on them has long since disappeared. There are bottles missing labels. The metal utility shelves most of the chemicals rest on are badly discolored and rusted in many places. The wooden shelving looks charred in places. There are thick layers of dust on many jars and bottles.

You ask Emmit why the storage room is in such a poor state and whether much of what is there shouldn't be removed. He says that about 70% of what is there should be disposed of. You ask why it hasn't been done before now. He says that the chemicals there can't simply be thrown into the dumpster and that there was never any money for proper disposal. You ask what it would take to have everything cleaned up properly. He says that there is a firm in the next state that specializes in removing and disposing of unwanted chemicals in an environmentally safe way. He tells you that he has long been concerned about the matter, but nothing has ever been done. There is a great deal of paperwork involved in disposing of unwanted chemicals.

Another concern of Emmit's is that there is no way to lock the storage area doors. Because of fire safety codes, all the classrooms along this side of the building have communicating doors that cannot be blocked or locked. Since the science storage room is between two classrooms, anyone who gets into any of the rooms on this side of the hall can enter it. Emmit goes on to say that anyone with even a rudimentary knowledge of explosives could find enough material in this room to blow the school up many times over. Someone just casually mixing chemicals would almost certainly create a poisonous gas. There was once an acid storage cabinet, but it fell apart as a result of exposure to the materials stored in it. There has never been a corrosives cabinet.

Furthermore, most of what is here should never have been ordered for a high school in the first place. The same principles and outcomes that used to be demonstrated with potentially dangerous compounds can be demonstrated just as effectively with much safer ones. When Emmit first came to this school, he had to retrain several members of his department to eliminate the use of several hazardous substances. He also taught them what to order. He has done numerous workshops elsewhere on laboratory safety.

This information leaves you surprised. There seems to be a serious problem here that has never been addressed. Emmit Mulvaney obviously has considerable expertise that has never been applied.

You ask what else the science department needs. He tells you that, except for the advanced placement classes, virtually every lab in the school is overcrowded, exceeding state legal limits, not by just one or two students, but by 35–50%. In addition, nearly half the gas jets do not work, and each microscope must be shared by four students because so many are no longer usable. He hasn't been able to get more because the inoperable ones still show up on the inventory. Two labs have chemical shower baths that do not work, three have ventilators that cannot be used, several of the sinks no longer function, and the list goes on and on.

You ask why he hasn't done anything to correct those problems. He says that he always includes the necessary repairs in his budget requests but that those items are simply eliminated. You ask why he hasn't fought for the funds he needs to maintain the laboratory facilities. He says he did for a while but no one seemed to listen to him. He says you are the first administrator who has ever even asked him about such things.

Case Questions

1. How serious is the problem with the chemical storage area?
2. What would you have expected the head of the science department to have done about the situation before now?

3. What do you feel is the reason Emmit Mulvaney hasn't taken more action to correct the situation?

4. What immediate actions do you plan to take?

5. How do you plan to deal with Emmit?

6. If you conclude that the science labs and equipment are in serious need of attention, how will you begin to rectify the situation?

7. Now that you are aware of the problems with the storage room, if someone breaks in tonight and causes a chemical explosion and fire, can you be held legally responsible?

8. How would you determine the priority of each problem to be corrected in the science department?

9. What long- and short-range goals will you establish, and how will you achieve them?

10. How will you present these concerns to the central office and the school board?

SUGGESTED ACTIVITY: List in order of priority the problems that need to be addressed in this case. Develop a written plan for correcting them and a strategy for presenting the plan to the board.

PROBLEM 37—HELPING YOUR TEACHERS SOLVE PROBLEMS: DEVELOPING THEIR DECISION-MAKING SKILLS

A. Paula Sponauer, who teaches math in your building, has come to ask your advice. A colleague for whom she has little respect has been assigned a student teacher. He is receiving a stipend for training the student. Mrs. Sponauer states that, for the first two weeks, the cooperating teacher told Rachael, the student teacher, just to observe in his classroom. The third week, he gave her papers to correct and said she could begin planning lessons for the second-period class for the following week. The following Monday, the cooperating teacher told Rachael that he would continue teaching second period because the class had entered a critical phase of instruction. Rachael is feeling frustrated, and her anxiety level is rising. She asked her cooperating teacher for more responsibility, but he said she wasn't ready. When Mrs. Sponauer asked him why he refused to turn even one class over to his student teacher, he responded that the best way for her to learn how to teach is by observing him. He said that if she were to take over the classroom, the students would lose too much time.

Rachael has been coming to Mrs. Sponauer for advice and feedback. She says she considers her cooperating teacher a jerk and has already told her university that she wants a new cooperating teacher. The university has not yet responded, but Mrs. Sponauer can see that Rachael is really struggling. Mrs. Sponauer wants to know how she should deal with Rachael and her colleague. She is willing to take Rachael as her student teacher. Mrs. Sponauer is a trained cooperating teacher.

Case Questions

1. What questions come to your mind as you listen to Mrs. Sponauer?
2. Under what circumstances and in what way would you choose to become directly involved in this situation?
3. If you choose to investigate the situation, how will you go about it?
4. What will you do if you find that Mrs. Sponauer's description is essentially accurate?
5. What will you do if you believe that Mrs. Sponauer has an ulterior motive for her actions?
6. In general, what should your relationships be with student teachers, cooperating teachers, university supervisors, and the university placing students in your school?
7. What unstated factors may make this a serious problem?
8. How would you compare this problem with the one presented in Chapter 1, problem 13, part F?

B.   Stephen Mendyka is a veteran social studies teacher who has come to you during his prep period because of his concern about a student. Karl Pranski, the oldest of four children, has been a straight-A student since kindergarten, is well mannered, and obeys all rules to the letter. Now that he is in his senior year, it is anticipated that he will be valedictorian. He is president of the student council and president of the National Honor Society. He has earned three letters in soccer and two in tennis. He is respected but not popular. He works part-time in a supermarket. He has already been accepted at Annapolis. Mr. Mendyka has had Karl twice in class. Karl works very hard but seems to be humorless and lacking in imagination and creativity.

Last weekend Karl's father was burned to death when the car he was driving slammed into a telephone pole. Karl was absent the morning of the funeral but reported to school at noon. Mr. Mendyka offered Karl condolences, but his reply was that his father's death was no great loss to anyone. As usual, Karl showed no emotion. Your teacher feels that something is very wrong, but he doesn't understand what it is. He wants to know what you think he should do.

Case Questions

1. What suspicions do you have about Karl and his family? Why? Is there anything you can and should do?
2. What advice will you give Stephen Mendyka?
3. How do you want your teachers to make referrals when students need help in their personal lives?

4. How much and what sort of training, if any, should teachers be given to help them spot signs of social and emotional problems in their students?

C. Laura Copeland teaches English. She was just about to leave school for the day when a student came into her room. Ms. Copeland recognized her as someone she had had in class two years ago, but it took her a while to remember that the student's name is Debbie. Ms. Copeland recalls her as a very shy, quiet, average student who seldom contributed anything in class. She had tried to draw her out, but Debbie seemed so uncomfortable that she stopped. Aside from an occasional greeting in the hall, Debbie had not spoken to Ms. Copeland since she was in her class, and Ms. Copeland could not imagine what Debbie might want when she came into her room.

After a few awkward false starts, Debbie told her that she was her favorite teacher. Debbie said that she didn't know who else to talk to. Eventually she blurted out that she thinks she is pregnant. She had never been asked out on dates and she thought that if she allowed boys to have sex with her, they might start asking her out. They did, but only to have sex. Debbie said she only had sex with the boys for a few weeks before she decided it was a mistake and started refusing. She also claimed that she always had the boys use condoms, so she didn't think she'd catch anything or get pregnant.

Debbie said that she had not spoken to anyone else about this. Ms. Copeland was not sure how to respond. She told Debbie that she had to give the matter some serious thought, and she asked her to come back after school tomorrow and not to do anything drastic between now and then. Shortly after Debbie left, Ms. Copeland came to your office to ask your advice.

Case Questions

1. What possibilities come to your mind immediately?
2. What additional information, if any, should Ms. Copeland seek?
3. What do you think of the way Ms. Copeland has handled the situation up to this point?
4. What will you tell Ms. Copeland to do?

SUGGESTED ACTIVITY: List the sorts of concerns you believe teachers should bring to a high school principal and the sorts of concerns they should solve on their own or bring to the attention of the guidance counselors. Develop a strategy for training your faculty to be problem solvers.

PROBLEM 38—THE YEARBOOK: TRYING TO PROVIDE MORE FOR STUDENTS

Barbara Walsh is serving her fourth year as faculty adviser to the yearbook staff. The compensation she receives under her extra-duty contract works out to less than 50 cents an hour, but she was editor of the yearbook when she was a senior in high school, and she enjoys working with the students in that capacity.

To meet the final deadline, the remaining sections of the yearbook have to be mailed off by noon Saturday. It is now Friday evening. Eleven students have been working with Ms. Walsh since school was dismissed, and it is now after 8:00. All that is left to complete is the class prophecy and the class will. The vast bulk of each of those sections has been written, but there remain about a dozen members of the graduating class about whom nothing has been decided. Most of them are unpopular or shy students, and it is difficult to come up with amusing things to say about them that are not too insulting. The staff is brainstorming. Perhaps because everyone is tired and anxious to finish, many of the suggestions are off-color or bitingly sarcastic. Some of the suggestions are rather funny, and Ms. Walsh finds herself laughing at a few of the more imaginative ones even though they are inappropriate. Eventually all members of the class have been assigned an imaginary future, and all juniors have been left a legacy. Many of the last ones agreed on are bland and uninspired, but at least the task is finished.

Ms. Walsh declares that, in celebration of the completion of the yearbook, she is treating everyone to pizza and soft drinks. She phones in an order, chooses two students to accompany her when she picks up the food, and leaves the other nine students to straighten up the yearbook office. The students set to work, but Bette Ambler and Casey Pauling think some of the rejected pictures, captions, prophecies, and bequests are too funny to be lost to posterity. They substitute them for the less colorful ones the group agreed on. They keep the packet to be mailed to the printers as it is, but they make the substitutions in the duplicate copy that will be kept on file.

When Ms. Walsh and the two students return with the pizza and drinks, the office is in good order and everyone is in high spirits. As they eat, the students speculate about what the reaction might have been if certain pictures, quotes, and captions had not been deleted. By 10:00 all the students have left, and Ms. Walsh is cleaning up the remains of the celebration. Some juice has spilled, and when she picks up the packet that is to be taken to the post office, she notices that it is wet on the bottom. On opening the packet she discovers that all but the top sheets have been soaked through. She spreads the wet pages out on the table to dry and decides that she will mail the duplicate file copy, keeping the originals as the backup. She makes out a new envelope. In the morning she goes to the post office and mails the final pages. She goes back to the school and files the original pages, which have dried overnight. There is nothing more to do until the books arrive from the printer.

The yearbooks arrive later than scheduled. They are distributed to the seniors as they leave their final graduation practice and to many of the rest of the students immediately afterward. Within minutes, the superintendent, Ms. Walsh, and you start receiving complaints, both in person and over the phone, from outraged students, parents, and school board members. You make an announcement: all yearbooks that have been distributed are to be returned immediately, and no more are to be distributed.

You then call Ms. Walsh out of class and ask for an explanation. Ms. Walsh is visibly upset by what has happened. She immediately goes to the yearbook office, gets the duplicate copy of the material, and shows you that the offensive material is not there. She says she does remember that some inappropriate remarks were made during the last-minute silliness, but all of them were purged from the copy sent to the printers.

News of the ribald comments passes quickly around the school. Almost no yearbooks are returned, and the students who ordered yearbooks and have not yet received them are demanding theirs. The yearbooks in circulation become a valued commodity.

Later that afternoon Bette and Casey confess to you and Ms. Walsh that they substituted the biting pictures, prophecies, bequests, and captions for those agreed upon, but only in the office copy, not for publication. By that time some people are demanding that Ms. Walsh be fired, and others are talking about taking legal action. You phone the printers in Ms. Walsh's presence. The printers say that they only printed what they had been sent and that they have a release form, signed by Ms. Walsh, authorizing the printing. It would be mid-July at the earliest before revised yearbooks could be printed and ready for distribution.

You announce that a revised yearbook will be distributed over the summer and that all yearbooks already in circulation are to be returned immediately. Most of the students say that, since everyone already knows about the pictures and comments in question, a censored version is not needed. They say they ordered the yearbook with the understanding that it would be in their hands before the end of the school year so that they could get the autographs of the graduating seniors. They demand that the remaining yearbooks be distributed immediately. Whatever damage might be done has already been done, and the bulk of the publication is fine.

The superintendent repeatedly says that the matter is being taken care of at the building level without central office participation. The chairperson of the school board is calling for a special emergency meeting.

Case Questions

1. The specifics of the offensive pictures and remarks have been omitted here because standards vary so significantly from community to community. What sorts of pictures and remarks would have evoked this type of reaction in your community?

2. Do you anticipate the filing of legal actions in this case? If so, by whom, against whom, and on what basis?

3. What is your evaluation of Ms. Walsh's actions in this case? The superintendent's actions? Your own actions?

4. Is the reaction described likely to fade quickly?

5. What would you do now if you were Ms. Walsh? The superintendent?

6. What do you think is the most likely outcome of the emergency school board meeting if it is held? Do you think it will actually be held? How should the superintendent respond to the call for an emergency meeting?

7. Does Ms. Walsh have a sound defense if she relies on the constitutional guarantee of freedom of speech?

8. How will you deal with Bette and Casey?

9. Was it reasonable for Ms. Walsh to leave nine students unsupervised in the yearbook office? Was it wise to take two students with her to get pizza and soft drinks?

10. Is the underlying moral of this case that people who try to provide more for students outside the classroom are penalized?

SUGGESTED ACTIVITY: In a two-page paper, describe how a principal should supervise extracurricular activities.

PROBLEM 39—THE STATE ATHLETIC ASSOCIATION STANDARDS: MIGHT VERSUS RIGHT

Steve Clarke is the captain of the varsity basketball team, a senior, and an honor roll student. He is very popular. For the first time ever, your high school is in contention for the regional championship, and emotions are running high, not only in the school, but in the whole district. When the team made it to the finals, Steve borrowed his father's van and took his teammates out to celebrate. He picked up a case of beer. Steve did not drink any, but the other members of the team did. A few minutes after Steve bought the beer, state troopers pulled the van over and arrested Steve for possession, for serving minors, and for having an open container.

The charges constituted a clear violation of the State Athletic Association standards, and in accordance with the rules, the coach suspended Steve and two of his teammates from the team. Because Steve is one of your best players and the school is in the finals of the regional championship, the district is sharply divided over the elimination of Steve and the two other players. Some say that the matter should be handled in court, since it did not happen on school grounds. The date of the hearing is long after the date of the championship game. Others say that the principle of abiding by the rules should be upheld even if it costs the title. A few say that Steve just behaved like any other red-blooded American boy and that everyone is making a big deal out of nothing. Teens drink all the time, and it is foolish to pretend it doesn't happen or to penalize one of the best kids in school. Besides, one case of beer among so many boys wouldn't be enough to get any of them drunk.

The superintendent, the chairperson of the school board, and you all publicly support the coach's decision to suspend the three players. Privately the coach is very upset by what has happened. He feels that Steve betrayed him personally and put him in a position where he had no choice but to suspend the players. The incident is public knowledge throughout the athletic community. The coach tells you that if the kid had only waited until after the game, he might have bought them the beer himself.

The next day the coach is served with an injunction obtained by the parents of the three suspended boys. The injunction bars him from excluding Steve and the other two players, on the grounds that athletic scholarships are at stake. It requires him not only to reinstate the three players, but also to make sure they have their normal amount of playing time. The coach is furious. He had been sympathetic, but he sees the injunction as an affront to the integrity of high school sports and coaching discipline.

At 5:00 P.M. on the day of the championship game, the school board votes at a special meeting to disband the boys basketball team. The action is taken on the recommendation of the coach, with the endorsement of the superintendent.

Case Questions

1. What is your assessment of the court's role in this case?
2. Are athletic association regulations enforceable?
3. What do you think of the coach's reaction?
4. Evaluate the superintendent's response. How would you have responded if you were in his position?
5. Is the matter now at an end? What do you envision will happen next?
6. Was the board action legal?
7. How will you respond?
8. If asked for a statement, what will you tell the press?

SUGGESTED ACTIVITY: Seek expert opinion on how binding athletic association regulations are.

PROBLEM 40—INTEGRATING THE 10TH-GRADE CURRICULUM: WORKING COOPERATIVELY TO PROMOTE CHANGE

Dr. Jerry Fengler has recently been hired as coordinator of secondary curriculum, a position both you and the superintendent had been urging the school board to create for some time. The strongest recommendations made by the visiting team at the time of your last reaccreditation were that the curriculum be coordinated and that a humanities program be established. Jerry was given that responsibility. You gave him the information and suggestions you had, pledged your support, and determined that, although you would monitor progress, you would stay out of the process of program development.

Jerry spent several days reviewing the existing curriculum materials, the state guidelines, and the literature on humanities programs. He then spoke to most of the faculty, either at department meetings or individually. As Jerry listened to what people had to say, he quickly became aware that the primary obstacles both to creating a humanities program and to integrating curriculum were the territorial isolation of the high school staff and the question of control of turf. Those were the obstacles he had suspected he would find.

He decided the best way to accomplish both goals was to combine them and create an integrated humanities pilot program that had a good chance of success. A quick review of the existing course offerings convinced him that the 10th-grade college prep courses, called 10 C, naturally lent themselves to a humanities program. The typical 10 C student took Biology 10 C, the second year of a foreign language, World History C, English 10 C (which was primarily world literature), geometry, and something called Core 10. Core 10 met daily and alternated a fine arts class with a physical education class—one semester of art appreciation, one semester of music appreciation, and a full year of physical education, which met on the days art or music did not. A typical sophomore earned a quarter credit of art appreciation, a quarter credit of music appreciation, and a half credit of physical education by the end of the year.

When Jerry reviewed the faculty who normally taught the 10 C courses, the selection did not seem so promising. There were only two weak teachers within the group, but there were several who were known to guard their sovereignty over their classrooms jealously. In addition, four people taught English 10 C, and three people taught the upper track in World History. Jerry decided that, if the pilot were to succeed, he needed a small core of solid teachers who could work together closely. There were six sections of English 10 C and seven sections of World History C. One teacher taught all the art appreciation, and another taught all the music appreciation. Jerry wanted one teacher to teach five sections of English 10 C and another to teach five sections of World History C. The remaining sections of those courses would not be included in the pilot and could therefore serve as a control group. To those sections the school would assign students who were taking classes out of sequence, students who were taking AP courses, and students who had other scheduling irregularities.

Jerry spoke with several faculty members and identified the teachers he wanted for the English and history slots in the pilot. There was no choice about the art and music appreciation teachers, but they were not expected to pose any particular obstacle to the creation of a new program. Working with you and the head of guidance, Jerry devised a master schedule that provided for the teaching assignments he wanted. No one felt that the physical education, math, and science departments would be affected, so no provision was made for them.

Under the tentative schedule, the students assigned to each of the five pilot sections of English 10 C would remain intact as a class for World History and for music and art appreciation. Although the students could choose which foreign language to take, they would be assigned to foreign-language class sections composed exclusively of students included in the pilot population. With that much of the students' schedules determined, the geometry, Biology C, and physical education class sections were virtually identical in student membership to the corresponding English 10 C sections.

Once a tentative master schedule and mock class rosters were established, Jerry approached the faculty members who would be teaching the targeted 10 C classes. The school board had agreed to offer those staff members a modest stipend for the additional work of developing a new program. Some of the faculty members who had been displaced were given such perks as permission to attend conferences, a voice in what their new assignments would be, and grant money for the purchase of equipment and supplies.

The way was cleared for the development of the new program. Jerry had decided that the World History C curriculum map would serve as the skeletal foundation for the humanities program. The reconstructed master schedule would give the faculty the freedom to team-teach, combine classes, and double or even triple periods. Jerry provided the team members with samples of curricula from other schools and a variety of articles on developing humanities programs. By consensus, the teachers who would be assigned to the humanities program agreed to meet every Tuesday afternoon for an hour after school.

The first two meetings of the team were not very productive. It was mid-fall, and the program was not to be initiated until the following academic year. The team struggled to establish the ground rules for the operation of the group, to clarify the task before them, and to understand exactly what was meant by a humanities program. They repeatedly assumed that they couldn't change things that had been common practice for many years. Jerry had to continually assure them that they had a great deal of flexibility and could let their creative energies flow. He had a difficult time convincing them that the group really had the authority to make substantial changes. The only requirement was that the established curricular content had to be covered.

By the third meeting, the 10 C team–an English teacher, a history teacher, an art teacher, a music teacher, a Latin teacher, a Spanish teacher, a French teacher, and a German teacher–had found an identity and established a working relationship. Both were to evolve over time, but the foundation remained solid. Skepticism virtually disappeared, and the ideas began to flow rapidly. The group's first significant decision was to eliminate separate semesters for art appreciation and music appreciation. Both courses would meet for the same number of class periods as before, but the instruction would be stretched over the whole year. The second decision was that each term each student would complete a major research-oriented project, which would receive a grade from each of the disciplines. The team investigated possibilities for joint field trips and even worked to persuade a nearby college's drama department to perform certain major works in the high school. The team agreed to exchange lesson plans with each other, develop joint lesson plans, meet weekly to exchange views, offer each other mutual support, evaluate the program, plan for both the immediate and the long-range future of the program, and discuss students as needed.

Jerry had anticipated that the initial flush of energy and enthusiasm would level off as the group moved into working out specifics. That was not the case. Each teacher did, however, block out some time to cover material that did not integrate itself readily with the overall program. Initially the team had planned to integrate everything, but once they began examining what they needed to cover, they decided that some things needed to be done in the traditional way. Once that was determined, they were amazed how much of their material they could integrate easily.

Jerry kept the entire faculty updated by issuing periodic bulletins to them about the progress of the group. The bulletins were realistic and discussed the problems as well as the things that were falling into place neatly. Jerry asked the student newspaper to report on the committee's work. He wrote articles for the local press. The central office and the school board were also kept informed.

In February a few parents asked to see what had been developed to date. Some of the parents were hostile to the idea of creating a humanities core of courses. After they met with the team, their objections were greatly diminished. One of the parents became involved with the committee and provided useful feedback and ideas.

In March the team was unexpectedly approached by one of the physical education teachers, who proposed the idea of developing a unit on the significance of organized sports in international relations. She proposed a school Olympic competition with many of the same contests as the ancient Olympic games. The geometry teacher came forward and offered to do a series of lessons demonstrating how knowledge of geometry in the ancient world was necessary for the building of the pyramids in Egypt, Latin America, and Southeast Asia. The lessons would point out how differences among those cultures in their levels of understanding of geometry produced variations in what they built. He then developed a second series of lessons on the ancients' use of geometry in navigation and in the development of the principles of logic. One of the biology teachers decided she would incorporate lessons illustrating how a knowledge of anatomy allowed artists to depict people and animals more accurately, how lack of sanitation spread diseases during the Middle Ages, and how medical science has greatly extended the life span of 20th-century human beings.

By the end of the school year, the plans had been finalized and approved by the school board. The 10 C faculty was ready, the community was at least mildly supportive, and the students' interest had been piqued.

Case Questions

1. What should Jerry do to maintain the high level of enthusiasm for the program over the summer?
2. What steps should you take to ensure the pilot has the greatest chance to succeed? What can Jerry do?
3. How should the new humanities program be initiated and supervised?
4. How should the program be evaluated?
5. At what point should Jerry begin to withdraw from his central position in this program? How should he accomplish that withdrawal?
6. If the pilot project goes well, what must happen for the humanities program to be sustained at the 10 C level and expanded to the entire 10th grade? Is the expansion a good idea? Is it possible?
7. What are the key factors in determining whether this approach will fail or succeed in the long run?
8. What might have induced you, as principal, to take a more active part in this project?

SUGGESTED ACTIVITY: Chronicle the steps Jerry took in the development of the humanities program. Decide whether you would have taken the same steps. If so, why? If not, what would you have done differently?

CHAPTER SUMMARY

About the background: In any school system formed by court action, there is a period of turmoil and adjustment. In a district such as this one, which was created specifically to cross ethnic neighborhoods, urban-suburban-rural lines, political boundaries, and socioeconomic demarcations, tension is seldom far below the surface, even when the initial shock is long past.

All high schools have cliques, and large high schools tend to have more and stronger cliques. The groupings in this school are probably so structured that very few students can interact socially with more than one group or can change cliques easily. The groups most likely to be open to new members are cliques revolving around substance abuse. Social identity is very powerful in such a setting. You can often identify group members by the way they dress or wear their hair. The cliques will be most readily apparent in the cafeteria. Students learn the first day where they can and cannot sit. If a social group expects its members not to do well academically and to adopt antisocial behaviors, the members will do whatever is necessary to uphold that standard. It takes great courage to challenge peer traditions.

Teachers may be only slightly less clique-oriented than the students. In large schools the members of each department generally keep to themselves, and there may be gender and ethnic groupings as well. Communications in large schools are different from those in smaller schools. Some segments of the community get information much earlier than others, and certain parts of the population remain entirely uninformed about some issues. The segmentation of both the student population and the teacher population is enforced in part by strict tracking and specialization of functions. Students in honors and advanced placement courses do not know the other college preparatory students, and each of the other tracks is equally isolated. The only common ground is physical education.

In smaller schools up to 70% of the student body is involved in extracurricular activities. In large schools, although there may be many more activities offered, only 10–15% of the population participates. That phenomenon contributes to the impersonal nature of the school and the lack of interaction. The large geographic area makes participation more difficult. Some students must spend more than 2 hours a day on the bus. All after-school activities from detention to sports depend on the availability of late buses and create situations in which large numbers of students are waiting for activities to start or for a ride home. Those situations create an additional supervision problem, as do the large number of student cars such schools have. The transportation problem also effectively eliminates some students from some activities.

Because the school district crosses several political boundaries, the community resources available to the students differ enormously. After-school employment opportunities are different, and even scholarships for postsecondary education may be tied to where students live. No community identifies with a high school such as the one described, and civic pride in the school is probably minimal. Such schools are much more likely to suffer vandalism than schools that are an integral part of a community.

In schools closely associated with a community, the high school principal often vies with the superintendent for social prominence and name recognition. In metropolitan areas, school administrators are far less well recognized outside the school setting.

A high school principal is expected at least to put in an appearance at most school functions and sporting events. It is on such occasions that parents have the greatest informal access to the principal. The need to attend so many functions lengthens the principal's workday and workweek. It is usual for high school principals to average 60–70 hours a week during the school year. Only in July is there a significant decrease in workload. By August the pressures of the next school year have caused the load to pick up again.

In this chapter, the principal seems to have a great deal of direct contact with teachers and students. That is unusual for a school so large. In such a setting it is easy for the chief building administrator to be isolated. The principal must have worked to establish a very high profile. That means that the administrative details that allow the school to function must have been delegated to others. Since two of the vice principals vied unsuccessfully for the position and are actively seeking principalships elsewhere, the new principal may have to monitor their functioning carefully to make sure they continue to complete their assigned duties promptly and well. It would be only human for such persons to turn their focus to job hunting and away from their present responsibilities. The best possible outcome would be for both vice principals to find suitable positions elsewhere. Since one assistant principal was the popular choice among the faculty, the new principal should be tactful and very professional in order to establish himself or herself as the primary educational leader of the school.

In larger systems, the lines of authority are more complex, and roles are more specific. In general, a review of the statewide educational directory will show that as a system grows larger the number of administrators rises exponentially. The climate in large systems is often more formal, and the bureaucracy sometimes takes on an authority and identity of its own. Turf issues surface, and ownership frequently becomes more cautiously protected. Leadership by means of personality and human interrelationship becomes much more difficult as people identify more closely with specific segments of the total system and as networks of alliances are formed. An us-versus-them atmosphere often predominates.

Most of the problems in chapter 3 deal with a principal's relationships, often confrontational, with other people within the school community. In a large school, when an administrator deals with one teacher, the entire faculty often feels threatened. In schools where no teacher's performance has been challenged for some time, there is comfort in thinking "I must be safe if no one has confronted them, because they are obviously so much weaker than I am." The lack of regular contact that is possible in a large school, combined with the strong union that is probable in such a school, can lead to the teachers' alienation from the administration. Those considering becoming chief administrators of large facilities must understand the difference in dynamics from smaller systems and must be prepared to adjust their approaches accordingly. In a small system it may be possible to establish warm friendships with colleagues. In a larger system it is much more difficult.

High school principals usually receive more pay than their colleagues in middle and elementary schools, but along with the higher pay comes the need to appear at many more nighttime school and community functions, supervise larger staffs and more students, and deal with more complex structures. In the not-too-distant past, the high school principalship was a mandatory step toward the superintendency. That is less true now. Many elementary principals are now moving on to the superintendency, and in some parts of the country, superintendents are selected from among candidates with business backgrounds. Those trends reflect the changing nature of central office administration and the general population's perception of what a superintendent can and should be.

I must emphasize, however, that although the problems in this chapter are purposely more complex than those in the two previous chapters, the reader should not infer that principals of elementary and middle schools do not also face complex and difficult problems or that high school administrators do not face situations similar to the ones described in the earlier chapters.

Perhaps the most difficult role for a principal to sustain is that of chief curriculum leader. The demands on a principal are usually such that it is very difficult to keep track of developments in the curriculum area. Curriculum is at the heart of education, and although in a large system there may be department heads and a curriculum director to do the major part of the work in that domain, the principal must have at least a nodding acquaintance with developments in the field and must be able to oversee those who have more direct responsibility. In this chapter, for example, we have seen how a principal's knowledge of industrial arts, art, and home economics can come into play.

SUMMARY QUESTIONS

1.   What relationship should teachers and principals have? Should it vary between large and small schools? Between elementary and secondary schools?

2.   Do you think it would be easier or harder to establish yourself as the principal if you came up through the ranks of the school instead of coming from outside the system?

3.   Research indicates that the most effective principals are highly visible principals. In a school as large as this one, can you be highly visible, or is it necessary to spend most of your time in the office?

4.   What would you choose to delegate to your four assistant principals? Would you delegate differently to the two who had been candidates for your position?

5.   One of your assistant principals was the candidate of choice of your teachers. Does that complicate your efforts to establish yourself as the school's educational leader? If so, in what way?

6.   When it became clear that you must request the termination or nonrenewal of the contract of a tenured teacher, under what circumstances would you elect to press the teacher into resigning rather than go through the firing process?

7.   What is the effect on the rest of the staff when a tenured teacher is either dismissed or forced to resign? How would you handle the staff reaction?

8.   What sort of relationship should the principal of a very large school have with the students? When should the principal become involved with discipline?

9.   Would you elect to have regular administrative team meetings?

10.   How involved should your assistant principals be in the decision-making process?

11.   What should the role of the principal be with regard to curriculum development, implementation, and evaluation?

SUGGESTED READING

Alexander, K. (1980). *School law.* St. Paul, MN: West.

Anderson, B. F. (1980). *The complete thinker: A handbook of techniques for creative and critical problem solving.* Englewood Cliffs, NJ: Prentice-Hall.

Begel, D. (1990). Using high school sports as a positive public relations tool. *NASSP Bulletin, 74*(530), 28–32.

Black, J., & English, F. (1986). *What they don't tell you in schools of education about school administration.* Lancaster, PA: Technomic.

Boyer, E. L. (1983). *A report on secondary education in America.* New York: Harper & Row.

Castetter, W. (1986). *The personnel function in educational administration* (4th ed.). New York: Macmillan.

Cookson, P. W., Sadovnik, A. R., & Semel, S. F. (1992). *International handbook of educational reform.* Westport, CT: Greenwood Press.

Cruickshank, D. R. (1980). *Teaching is tough.* Englewood Cliffs, NJ: Prentice-Hall.

Darder, A. (1991). *Culture and power in the classroom: A critical foundation for bicultural education.* Westport, CT: Bergin & Garvey.

Drake, T., & Roe, W. (1986). *The principalship.* New York: Macmillan.

Dunn, K. J., & Dunn, R. S. (Eds.). (1983). *Situational leadership for principals: The school administrator in action.* Englewood Cliffs, NJ: Prentice-Hall.

Genck, F. H. (1991). *Renewing America's progress: A positive solution to school reform.* Westport, CT: Praeger.

Glickman, C. D. (1989). *Supervision of instruction: A developmental approach* (2nd ed.). Boston, MA: Allyn & Bacon.

Glover, G. J. (1994). The hero child in the alcoholic home: Recommendations for counselors. *School Counselor, 41*(3), 185–190.

Goodlad, J. (1971). *A place called school.* New York: McGraw-Hill.

Kepner, C. H., & Tregoe, B. B. (1965). *The rational manager: A systematic approach to problem solving and decision making.* New York: McGraw-Hill.

Lightfoot, S. L. (1983). *The good high school.* New York: Basic Books.

Maeroff, G. I. (1988). *The empowerment of teachers: Overcoming the crisis of confidence.* New York: Teachers College Press.

Magill, J. F. (1983). Thoughts about school and community sports programs. *PTA Today, 8*(5), 20.

Medley, D. M. (1984). *Measurement-based evaluation of teacher performance: An empirical approach.* New York: Longman.

Metz, M. H. (1986). *Sources of workers' subculture in organizations: A case study of public school faculty.* Madison, WI: University of Wisconsin, School of Education, National Center on Effective Secondary Schools.

Morris, W. C., & Sashkin, M. (1976). *Organization behavior in action: Skill building experiences.* St. Paul, MN: West.

Newell, C. (1978). *Human behavior in educational administration.* Englewood Cliffs, NJ: Prentice-Hall.

O'Reilly, R. C., & Green, E. T. (1992). *School law for the 1990s: A handbook.* Westport, CT: Greenwood.

Ornstein, A. C., & Hunkins, F. P. (1988). *Curriculum: Foundation, principles and issues.* Boston, MA: Allyn & Bacon.

Pruitt, D. G., & Rubin, J. Z. (1986). *Social conflict: Escalation, stalemate, and settlement.* New York: Random House.

Sergiovanni, T. J. (1991). *The principalship: A reflective practice perspective* (2nd ed.). Boston, MA: Allyn & Bacon.

Schultz, F. (Ed.). (1994). *Multicultural education 94/95.* Guilford, CT: Dushkin Publishing Group.

Sizer, T. R. (1984). *Hoarce's compromise: The dilemma of the American high school: The first report from a study of high schools.* Boston, MA: Houghton Mifflin.

Snyder, K. J. (1986). *Managing productive schools: Toward an ecology.* Orlando, FL: Academic Press College Division.

Stover, D. (1988). What to do when grown-ups want to spoil the fun of school sports. *American School Board Journal, 175*(7), 19-22.

Swift, E. M. (1991). Sports in a school curriculum: Four postulates to play by. *Teachers College Record, 92*(3), 425–432.

Tanner, D., & Tanner L. (1987). *Supervision in education: Problems and Practices.* New York: Macmillan.

Thomson, S. D. (Ed.). (1993). *Principals for our changing schools: The knowledge and skill base.* Fairfax, VA: National Policy Board for Educational Administration.

Valente, W. D. (1987). *Law in the schools.* New York: Macmillan.

Wiles, J., & Bondi, J. (1989). *Curriculum development: A guide to practice* (3rd ed.). New York: Macmillan.

Wood, C., Nicholson, E., & Findley, D. (1985). *The secondary school principal: Manager and supervisor.* Boston, MA: Allyn & Bacon.

Worthen, B. R., & Sanders, J. R. (1973). *Educational evaluation: Theory and practice.* Belmont, CA: Wadsworth.

Yaffe, E. (1982). High school athletics: A Colorado story. *Phi Delta Kappan, 64*(3), 177–181.

Yohe, B., & Dunkleberger, G. (1985). The chemical storage dilemma: A workable solution. *Journal of Chemical Education, 62*(10), 876–878.

Zais, R. (1976). *Curriculum: Principles and foundation.* New York: Harper Collins.

Chapter

4

......

Daily Problems of
the Central Office

BACKGROUND

Marsden North is a large, primarily rural school district that takes in the northern half of Marsden County. The largest town in the district and the county is St. Stephen, the region's shopping and business center. The rest of the district consists of scattered villages. Agriculture and lumber are the two main sources of income. There are a few small lumber mills and one modest-sized paper mill. Aside from a few machine shops, the only other industry in the area is a doll factory in St. Stephen. About 15 years ago some of the local leaders tried to develop the area into a vacation spot, but the idea was met with indifference, and very little came of their efforts.

The population of Marsden County is very stable. Most families have lived in the area for several generations. To the casual observer, Marsden County seems to be a picturesque area with quaint little villages. The people who really know the county could tell you that if you go down almost any of the dirt roads that seem to wander everywhere, you will find battered, rusted trailers and dilapidated old farmhouses filled with the rural poor. More than 40% of Marsden North's population receives some sort of public assistance. Most of the rural poor have lived on the edge of society for generations. They live by subsistence farming, poaching, odd jobs, and barter. Food stamps have become a second currency for them, and alcoholism is epidemic among them. This part of the population has created a tightly bound, closed society of its own. Very few of their children ever finish high school, and most of the girls have had at least one baby by the time they reach 16. There are virtually no minorities in Marsden County.

The school district has six elementary schools. The smallest one has 71 students, and the largest, St. Stephen Elementary, has a few more than 600. Until 20 years ago each of the elementary schools, except St. Stephen, was a school for grades 1–12. There were no kindergartens. At that time, after much bitter debate, the district voted to build a regional junior–senior high school and make the old St. Stephen High School a regional vocational center. The total student population is just under 2,200.

Each school has its own school board, and a superboard made up of all members of all the other boards deals with central office affairs. The central office staff consists of a superintendent, an assistant superintendent, a business manager, a director of pupil personnel services, and three secretaries.

The superintendent has been in the position for 11 years and has the political and popular backing to remain in that post indefinitely. There have been several assistant superintendents; the present one is new to the district. The business manager has been there even longer than the superintendent and is the only native in the central office. The director of pupil personnel services has been there 3 years. In the problems that follow, you will assume the role of each of the four administrators for various exercises.

PROBLEM 41—THE SNOWSTORM: A CRISIS SITUATION

Part 1—The No-Win Decision

You were just hired as the new assistant superintendent. You took up your post on January 1. It is the last week of January. The superintendent recently completed the budget, in preparation for the districtwide school board meeting on the second Tuesday in February, and is taking a week-long vacation to Bermuda, leaving you in charge.

The weather forecast for today was for heavy snow beginning at noon and continuing well into the night, with significant accumulation possible. Several parents have called already asking if school will be closed early. You told them it is too early to know because the storm has not yet arrived. If school is to be closed, it will be announced on the local radio station. You know that by contract you must give the bus company one hour's notice of any early dismissal. You also know that if you do dismiss early, many children will be going home to empty houses. In addition, the head of the county road crew has called you to say that, once the storm starts, they will do the bus routes first and that if you close early his trucks will not have had a chance to sand the roads. Virtually all the district's students ride buses.

At 11:00 you phone the district to the west, the direction from which the storm is expected to come. You are told that it is not yet snowing there. Even to close the schools one hour early, you must make the decision before noon because the high school dismisses at 2:10. The buses must make the high school run first and then go back for the elementary students. You decide not to close early. You hope the storm will hold off for a few more hours. You call all the building principals and the local radio station to inform them of your decision.

Promptly at noon the first flakes begin to fall. By 12:15 the snow has become heavy and the wind has picked up. By 12:30 the roads are completely covered. You call the county public works department and find out that the trucks are already out sanding. Although there is nothing more you can do, the rest of the afternoon your office is flooded with calls from people who want to know if school has been canceled, what evening activities are canceled, and when they can expect their children home. Some of the calls are from angry parents who feel you should have closed the schools early.

At 3:45 you get a call from a very angry mother who says that she had been watching from her window, waiting for her 6-year-old to get home, and she saw bus 13 slide off the road entirely. Fortunately, no one was hurt, but you behaved very irresponsibly in not sending the students, at least the elementary ones, home early. She says that if the superintendent hadn't been away, this never would have happened. Perhaps the district should rethink its decision to hire you. You phone the bus company, which is in contact with the bus through radio, and learn that there are still nine students left on bus 13 and that it is stuck in a shallow ditch. None of the children are hurt, nor is the driver.

Case Questions

1. Did you make the right decision by not closing school?
2. What if you had closed school and the storm had not begun until later?
3. What factors weighed in your decision?
4. How should you handle the distressed mother who reported the accident?
5. What can you do now?

Part 2—Meanwhile, in West Clayton

West Clayton Elementary is one of the smaller schools in the district, and one of the most isolated. There is no principal, just a head teacher, John Farber. Because West Clayton is so far from the regional high school, two buses bring the high school students to West Clayton Elementary and then take all the West Clayton children home.

Today bus 16 left without incident. The driver of the second bus, bus 28, is Barney Frankfurter. Barney has been driving buses for 15 years, has always been dependable, and has a perfect driving record. Last weekend, however, Barney's wife left him, and Barney has been drinking heavily ever since. The high school students notice that the bus seems to be swerving on the way to West Clayton Elementary, but they attribute that to the icy roads. At West Clayton Barney loads all the students and begins his run to the farthest part of his route. Because of the storm, John tells his staff of four to leave as soon as the second bus has gone. They do, and John locks up the building and leaves immediately after.

About a mile and a half from the school, the bus skids out of control while going down a hill and comes to rest with one wheel in a ditch. Frank Woods, an 11th-grade honor student, takes charge and tells all the students to stay very still and be quiet. Barney Frankfurter is slumped over the wheel and is not moving. Frank gets his friend Karl to try to wake the driver. They cannot. Frank and Karl move Barney to the back of the bus and leave him on the floor. With Karl's help, Frank maneuvers the bus back onto the road and drives back to the school.

By the time the bus returns, West Clayton Elementary is locked and all the staff are gone. There is only one house nearby, and Karl walks over to it to use the phone but comes back saying no one was home. Frank goes around to the back of the building, trying to find some way to get inside. He decides to break the window of the third-and-fourth-grade room. He gets Karl to boost him up so that he can crawl in through the jagged, broken window. His left sleeve catches on the glass, and the glass makes a long, deep diagonal cut on the inside of his left arm. The cut is not painful and does not immediately begin to bleed. Frank pulls down the sleeve of his heavy, goosedown-filled coat, covering the cut. He also suffers a few other, minor lacerations.

Once inside, he unlocks the door and has all the children come inside. He tells them to call their parents to explain what has happened. Parents start arriving to get their children. Only after every child has phoned does Frank think to call the superintendent's office. You get the call, phone John Farber at home, and tell him to meet you as soon as possible at the school.

By the time you arrive at West Clayton Elementary, dusk is falling. You look quickly inside the open door of the bus and see no one. You go into the school. Most of the children have been picked up. Only Karl, Karl's two sisters, Frank and his brother, and one other student are left. Frank says he's very glad you're there. He's done everything he could and suddenly isn't feeling very well. You look at him and notice that the left sleeve of his coat is very dark and that there are traces of blood on his clothing. You ask him to take off his coat. It is obviously painful for him to do so. Once he does, you see the freely bleeding gash on his arm. Blood pours everywhere, and the saturated coat sleeve discharges some of what it has absorbed.

You immediately phone the hospital and tell them you are bringing in a 17-year-old male with a serious wound. You grab the blanket from the cot in the nurse's station and wrap Frank's arm. You tell Karl to call Frank's parents and tell them to meet you at the hospital immediately. You tell Karl to stay there until Mr. Farber arrives and to explain the situation to him. You bring Frank to your car. His younger brother insists on coming, and you agree. You go to the hospital as quickly as possible.

Case Questions

1. How would you evaluate Frank's actions?
2. Were you right to leave the office immediately to take charge of the situation?
3. Once you decided to drive to West Clayton, what might you have done before leaving the office?
4. What information should you have gotten from Frank when he called? What might you have instructed him to do?
5. How would you evaluate your actions up to the point where you discovered Frank's injury?
6. Was it wise to take Frank and his brother to the hospital?
7. Might you have handled the situation better?
8. Should you have left Karl in charge?

Part 3—Barney Frankfurter

Frank's mother is at the hospital when you arrive. You get Frank into emergency and phone West Clayton Elementary. John is there and reports that Karl and his sisters and the other student have just been picked up. He is cleaning up the broken glass in the classroom and making a temporary repair on the window. He asks if there is anything else he can to. You tell him to finish what he is doing, secure the building, and go home. You will call him there. You then call your office. Everyone has left except for the business manager, who says he will stay there until he hears from you again. You fill him in on what has happened. He says that, right after you left, the phone started ringing with people asking about the West Clayton situation. You tell him to call the bus company to have someone pick up the bus at the school.

By 6:00 Frank has been admitted to the hospital. He has lost a significant amount of blood, and the doctor tells you that if he had gone much longer, the loss would have become critical. He has 47 stitches on the inside of his left arm. There will be no permanent damage. You phone John and the business manager, tell them what has happened, and go home.

At 9:00 that evening the bus company drops a driver at West Clayton. The driver discovers Barney Frankfurter in the back of the bus. He is still unconscious. The driver takes the bus to the hospital. Barney has frostbitten fingers and toes. His blood alcohol content is still 0.21. The doctors estimate that at 3:00 p.m. it must have been well over 0.32. A reading of 0.08 is the legal level of drunkenness.

Several days later you receive notification that you and the district are being sued for leaving Barney exposed to the cold. He has lost six toes and four fingers to frostbite.

Case Questions

1. Did you act prudently once you arrived at the hospital?
2. What might you have done differently?
3. What obligation did you have to Barney? You contract for bus service; he is not a district employee.
4. What would you have said if a reporter had asked you for a statement at the hospital?
5. What, if anything, will you do about Frank and Karl?
6. How will you report this incident to the school board? To your superintendent?
7. Would it have been reasonable for you to suspect that Barney had an alcohol problem? If you had suspected it, what could you have done?

SUGGESTED ACTIVITY: Find out what the law is in your state concerning the admission of minors to hospitals for emergency medical treatment without parental permission.

PROBLEM 42—THE BUSINESS MANAGER: DEALING WITH A SUDDEN REVERSE

For the first two parts of this problem assume the role of the superintendent.

Part 1—An Unexpected Loss

The annual joint budget meeting was held last week, and everything went as well as expected. The only significant item that was defeated was the repaving of the high school parking lot. The vote to approve the budget was, however, much closer than it had been in the past. You are concerned that the trend might be to tighten the purse strings in the future. You are experiencing the usual relief after all the activity associated with preparing and passing the budget.

You have been in the office only a few minutes when your business manager's wife calls. With great difficulty she tells you that her husband died of a stroke very unexpectedly in his sleep last night. She says that she will contact you with details of the wake and funeral arrangements as soon as they are made, and she asks you to notify the appropriate people in the school system for her.

Your business manager was only in his mid-50s and seemed to be in good health. After you get over the initial shock of the news, you realize that over the years you have come to depend on him completely and have seldom worried about monetary matters. Your business manager always briefed you on finances and was at every meeting where budget questions were likely to arise. You had also become good friends.

Case Questions

1. Now that you have lost your business manager, what do you need to do immediately to make sure that financial matters continue to be attended to promptly?

2. How can you pick up the details that he had been working on and dropped so suddenly? How much do you need to find out about the daily financial operations? How closely involved should you become with those daily operations?

3. How will you go about replacing him?

4. What qualities are you going to look for in a new business manager?

5. What are you going to do until a new person can be hired?

Part 2—The Audit

After consulting your school boards, you decide that you must hire an outside auditor and an interim business manager. You make some phone calls to your contacts in the state department of education. They give you the name of a retired business manager who is highly recommended and who is willing to work a few months until you can find a permanent replacement. You already have a local auditor in mind. Between the auditor and the interim business manager, you feel that you can keep everything functioning nearly normally. You also resolve to maintain closer personal involvement in financial matters from now on.

The next few weeks are difficult and confusing. Aside from having to cope with a much higher level of turmoil than usual, you are grieving the loss of a friend.

The auditor, Laura Schofield, comes into your office one day and tells you that she has uncovered a serious problem. For the past several years, the former business manager had simply rolled over the debt on June 30, the end of your fiscal year, and had begun paying the faculty's summer salaries with next year's operating budget. It started 6 years ago, when he rolled over only a few thousand. He probably thought that he could make up the difference and end in the black the following June 30, but every year the amount rolled over has grown, and now nearly all of the July and August payroll has been coming from the new budget instead of the old one. That means you will have to find some way to pay nearly 14 months of teachers' salaries from a budget calculated to pay for 12 months. The only piece of good news is that a substantial portion of the faculty elected to receive their summer pay in a lump sum at the end of June and that their pay came out of the correct budget. What had looked like a modest surplus is suddenly a huge deficit.

You question Laura closely, and she says that she couldn't believe it at first either. It was done in such a straightforward way that it hadn't seemed possible. Every time she rechecked, however, she found the same thing. Laura reports that she has gone back over the past 7 years. Every penny is accounted for; there can be no question of anyone's having embezzled. The former business manager simply borrowed more and more from the budget for the following year.

The contractual date by which you must notify tenured staff that their positions may be eliminated is past, as is the date for notifying third-year probationary teachers that their contracts will not be renewed. The only faculty whose contracts you can choose not to renew for next year are first- and second-year probationary teachers. You have 3 days to notify the teachers who are in their second year.

Case Questions

1. What steps must you take immediately?
2. How will you inform your school boards?
3. Your budget for next year is now set. Is there anything you can do about it?
4. How will you inform your staff and faculty?
5. How will you deal with the press, who are sure to question you?
6. Two years ago your system went through reaccreditation. There was never a question about finances. How do you account for that?
7. You are scheduled to speak at the Rotary Club next Tuesday. You are sure to be besieged with questions then. How will you handle them?
8. This sort of news is bound to send shock waves through the school community. How can you minimize their negative impact? How can you keep morale from crumbling?
9. What is this likely to do to your professional reputation? You still have 16 months left on your contract. Should you start looking for another job? How do you decide about your professional future?
10. What ethical and moral obligations do you have to your dead friend and his family concerning his reputation and memory?

Part 3—The New Business Manager

You have just been hired as the new business manager. You have spent days going over the books with the auditor and the interim business manager. Everything is in as much order as possible, but you clearly have a huge deficit to contend with.

Case Questions

1. What measures will you take immediately?
2. What understandings and assurances do you want from the superintendent and the school boards?
3. How will you deal with the reputation of your predecessor?
4. How will you safeguard your own reputation?
5. What obligation do you owe the superintendent regarding that person's professional reputation and job security?

SUGGESTED ACTIVITY: Describe how a superintendent should monitor the functions of all central office personnel and should create a backup system for coverage of all essential functions in the event that the person normally responsible for them is incapacitated.

PROBLEM 43—THE FORGER: A FELON ON THE FACULTY

For this problem assume the role of the superintendent.

Part 1—Federal Marshals Wreck a Perfectly Good Friday Afternoon

Gary Hampton is one of the most popular teachers at the high school. He teaches printing, but he is also junior-varsity soccer coach and assistant track coach. He spends a great deal of time with students after school, working on all sorts of projects, and has been instrumental in keeping difficult-to-handle students out of trouble. He served time in prison for forgery, and he has used that experience in his volunteer work with juvenile offenders. He is also a member of the substance abuse task force and the adviser for an Explorer post, a coed program run by the Boy Scouts of America for high-school-aged students. Because of new state laws concerning the hiring of known felons, you supported him when it came time for him to renew his certification. Through your help, Gary was able to win an exemption from the new certification standards.

It is early Friday afternoon. Two federal agents come to your office. They tell you that they are about to arrest Gary for counterfeiting. They tell you that his former cellmate has been arrested for passing counterfeit bills and has implicated Gary as the source of the phony money. The news shocks you. You want to immediately deny it. The agents say that they don't want to cause a disturbance in the school, and they ask your cooperation in helping them make the arrest quietly. They are determined to arrest him on school grounds before he has a chance to flee. You say that he has last period free. The principal arranged Gary's schedule that way because of his two coaching assignments. The agents agree to wait 20 minutes, until the end of his last teaching period. They propose going in the shop entrance immediately after class and removing him with as few witnesses as possible. They ask you to come with them and to ask Gary to come outside for a word with you. Once he is outside, they plan to arrest him.

Case Questions

1. Will you comply with the agents' wishes?
2. What would be the likely outcome if you did not?
3. What are you going to tell the high school principal, the staff, the students, and the community? How will you do it?
4. If you agree to help the agents, will it appear that you assume Gary is guilty?
5. How are you going to deal with the school board and the media?

Part 2—The Reaction

The rumors and the reaction begin even before the car containing the arrested teacher has left school grounds. The immediate response, especially among the students, is anger, shock, and righteous indignation. The news and speculation about what has actually happened dominate the last period.

A massive expression of support for Gary materializes immediately. Several teachers say that the relationship he had with his former cellmate was negative and that, once caught, the man was probably only too happy to make a deal that would frame Gary or set him up. The juvenile offenders with whom Gary worked say this proves that the cops don't care who they arrest, as long as they can close the case, and that, no matter how long you stay out of trouble, when something happens the police always question ex-offenders first. Rather quickly, resentment grows against you. You are supposed to have set Gary up. The principal phones to say that he has been told that some students intend to sabotage your car.

As word of the incident spreads beyond the school community, some of the reaction begins to go the other way. An anonymous caller says that this is what you get for allowing known criminals to teach in our schools. The caller demands to know what other undesirable elements you are sheltering.

A sign appears in the faculty room asking for donations for the Gary Hampton defense fund. Students begin taking up a collection as well. The president of the school board phones, saying that she wants to call an emergency meeting to discuss the matter. She says that since the meeting is to discuss a personnel issue, it can be held in closed session. She wants the board to convene that evening.

Case Questions

1. What is your assessment of the situation?
2. How seriously do you take the talk of sabotaging your car? What will you do about that threat?
3. How do you respond to the collections being taken up for Gary by the students and teachers? May they collect money for such purposes on school grounds?
4. What do you expect the high school principal to do?
5. How do you respond to the anonymous caller? Do you anticipate additional calls in a similar vein?

6. What do you do about the emergency school board meeting?

7. If Gary asks to see or speak with you, what will you do?

Part 3—The School Board Action

When the school board meets that evening, it immediately goes into executive session. Two board members favor supporting Gary until and unless he is found guilty. One member wants to do nothing until the situation is more clear. The rest want to distance themselves from the case as much as possible. The strategy they prefer is to terminate Gary's contract immediately and disavow any knowledge of his former criminal record.

Case Questions

1. What legal grounds does the board have for terminating Gary's contract?

2. If Gary were acquitted after being fired, could he sue the district for back pay, damages, and reinstatement?

3. What impact is a decision to terminate Gary's contract likely to have on faculty and students, who are expressing overwhelming support for him?

4. What action would you recommend the board take now? What are the reasonable options open to the board?

SUGGESTED ACTIVITY: Prepare a brief statement for the press concerning the board's action in this case.

PROBLEM 44—THE DIVIDED SCHOOL BOARD: THE POLITICAL NATURE OF EDUCATION

For this problem, assume the role of the assistant superintendent.

Part 1—An Issue Is Created

Elmwood Elementary School has 84 students and four teachers. The local three-member school board is composed of two people who teach in other districts and one farmer. Because of the large number of evening meetings, the superintendent has assigned you the smaller districts. Having dealt with Elmwood for several months now, you can see that the smaller districts are not necessarily the easier ones. Elmwood has had disputes, reaching local crisis proportions, over whether one of the hot lunch workers could take the food scraps home to feed her pigs and whether the school should be required to use smaller garbage bags because the 70-year-old man who collects the garbage could no longer lift the larger ones. Those issues brought out so many people that the board meetings had to be moved into the community center bingo hall.

It has taken you until now to begin to understand that, for Elmwood, school board meetings are as much a source of social interaction as of decision making and that, to the people of Elmwood, the issues confronting the board are just as vital as those facing much larger schools. You have adjusted your thinking to the point where you understand that no matter is too trivial to become a problem for the board and no meeting will ever be canceled for lack of need.

The latest issue is whether to replace the freezer, sell it, do without it, or make do with it. As usual, the board is divided. The two teachers are taking the position that the freezer needs to be replaced. One of them wants to sell the existing freezer. The other wants to keep it for emergency backup and for use at the community Fourth of July picnic. The farmer, Henry Burke, says that the school can make do with the present freezer for a few more years and that he sees no real need for it anyway. It soon becomes apparent that the argument has very little to do with the freezer. Rather, it is a power struggle in a situation where there is almost no power to be had. It is nearly 11:00 p.m., and there are still three items left on the agenda.

Case Questions

1. How do you deal with this immediate situation?
2. Is there any long-range approach you can take to make the board into a functioning unit and put issues into a more reasonable perspective?
3. The other small boards you handle have brief, informal, practical meetings. They sometimes cancel meetings if there is nothing pressing to decide. The board members take turns bringing in refreshments and are pleasant to each other. What could be the reasons Elmwood is so different? Is this just a situation you must endure, or can you take some positive action?
4. Is there anything you can do if one of the other boards begins to argue the way Elmwood does?

Part 2—Proposed Board Reorganization

The Elmwood board adjourned without making any decision about the freezer and without taking any action on the other items on the agenda. Two days later you receive a letter from Sharon Oliver, the chairperson of the Elmwood board, submitting her resignation. She has mailed copies to her fellow board members, and each of them phones you. School board elections are only a month away, and Ms. Oliver has submitted her name for reelection.

Henry Burke says he is glad she resigned and says she should remove her name from the ballot. He says that he has filed a petition with the town clerk, asking that the number of board members be raised from three to five. Mr. Burke just made the deadline for filing the petition. He says that Elmwood must get rid of the teachers on the board. He is pushing specific candidates to run for the seat now vacant and the two new seats. Mr. Burke says that there will then be four sensible votes and the one remaining teacher on the board, who can be voted out next year. He wants you to hold a special meeting to resolve the freezer issue, deal with the remainder of the old agenda, and appoint an interim replacement for the former chairperson. He thinks he should be appointed the new chair. Without giving you a chance to respond, Mr. Burke says he expects your support on this matter and hangs up.

Larry Martin, the other teacher on the board, says he has called Sharon Oliver and asked her to reconsider her resignation. She has done so and will be sending you and Mr. Burke a letter withdrawing her resignation. Mr. Martin says that the board should be kept to three members and that he has submitted a petition asking that Henry Burke be recalled. He asks what you think about this matter.

Case Questions

1. What immediate response do you give to Larry Martin?
2. How will you deal with the resignation and its withdrawal?
3. How will you deal with Henry Burke?
4. What will you do about the proposed special school board meeting?
5. What ethical, legal, and moral issues must you face?
6. Are you going to support anyone in this matter? Are you going to support the proposed board expansion?
7. Is it time to bring in the superintendent?
8. How will you keep this problem from absorbing all your time and energy?
9. What do you think would be the best possible outcome?

SUGGESTED ACTIVITY: Devise strategies for keeping school boards on task.

PROBLEM 45—THE ABUSED CHILDREN: THE LAW AND THE SCHOOL

For this problem put yourself in the place of the director of pupil personnel.

Part 1—The Abuse Is Discovered

Mary Ellen Tamworth's third-grade class has been doing a unit on health and personal safety. At the conclusion of the unit, she shows a film on what to do if someone tries to touch your body inappropriately. All through the unit Linda Morse has been unusually quiet and withdrawn. Partway through the film, Linda runs out of the room. Her teacher follows her. Linda is very upset, and Mary Ellen takes her to the school nurse. Eventually Linda tells the nurse that her brother Derrick, who is in the seventh grade, has been touching her and making her bleed. It hurts when he does it, but he said that if she told he would beat her up. The nurse gives Linda two biologically correct dolls and asks her to show her exactly what Derrick does to her. She indicates anal intercourse.

The nurse immediately calls Derrick's principal and you, asking you to come to the school as soon as possible. Just as you are leaving the building, Derrick's principal calls, asking you to come to the high school immediately. You phone the appropriate state agencies and report what the nurse has told you. Then you go to the high school, which is closer than the school Linda attends.

By the time you get to the high school, the police have phoned the principal and asked him to question Derrick before they get involved. The principal asks you to be present and to participate in the questioning. The principal calls Derrick into his office, and you begin by repeating what the nurse has told you about Linda. At first Derrick angrily denies everything. Then, quite suddenly, he starts to cry and says that he did it, but that is what boys are supposed to do to girls. It's what his stepfather does to him, and that's not right. He says that last year, when he was in sixth grade, he tried to tell the principal, but no one believed him. After that, his stepfather broke his arm and threatened to kill him if he ever said anything again. He wants you to protect him, because now he is terrified at the prospect of having to face his stepfather. You phone the nurse and the police and tell them what Derrick has just told you. The police instruct you to bring Derrick to the elementary school and not to release either child except into their custody.

You have the principal bring all Derrick's records and accompany you to the elementary school. The principal is reluctant to leave his building, but under the circumstances you refuse to transport Derrick alone. Both of you go. When you arrive at the elementary school, a state child welfare worker is there, questioning Linda and her teacher. You tell the worker what Derrick told you and what the police told you.

You leave Derrick with his principal and go to speak with the elementary school principal privately. She says that Derrick did make some sort of nonspecific complaint to her last year but that she could not understand what he was saying. When she pressed for details and clarification, he refused to say anything else and indicated that he had only said what he did to see how she would react. A few days later he come to school with his arm in a cast. He said he had broken his arm playing football. Derrick avoided the principal after that. You ask if that incident didn't make her suspicious that something serious was wrong. She replies that she felt there might be a problem but that she was waiting for more solid evidence before doing anything. Nothing more ever came of it, the year ended, and Derrick moved on to the high school.

Case Questions

1. Have you acted properly so far in this matter?

2. Is it appropriate for you to investigate this matter when it seems that the law has been broken? Why did the police want you to question Derrick before they became involved?

3. Did the elementary school principal act prudently? The high school principal? Mary Ellen Tamworth? The nurse?

4. What information concerning Linda and Derrick should you give the child welfare worker and the police? Is there any information that you cannot give them because of confidentiality?

5. What ethical, legal, and moral responsibility do you have toward Linda and Derrick? Toward your professional colleagues? Toward the district?

Part 2—The Police Arrive

When you have concluded your interview with the elementary school principal, you find that the high school principal has gotten a custodian to drive him back to his school. The state worker asks you to come into a room with Derrick. Derrick is crying very hard. The worker tells Derrick to remove his pants and underwear. He does. There are blood stains on the seat of his underwear. Derrick says his latest intimate contact with his stepfather was this morning before school. Derrick reports that he often bleeds from his rectum. Derrick gets dressed again.

The police arrive and speak in turn with the nurse, Linda, Derrick, the state worker, Mary Ellen Tamworth, the elementary school principal, and you. They phone the high school principal. The police ask you to be present when they question Linda and Derrick and to act in loco parentis. With some reluctance, you do. After what seems to be quite a long time, the police inform you they are taking Linda and Derrick into protective custody. They ask you to hand over both of the students' permanent records and to be prepared to testify in court.

Case Questions

1. How do you assess the high school principal's actions?
2. Was it appropriate for the state worker to have Derrick disrobe in front of you? Should you have permitted it?
3. Was it appropriate for you to be present in loco parentis when they questioned Linda and Derrick?
4. Can you legally hand over Linda and Derrick's permanent records? If so, under what circumstances?
5. What, if anything, do you tell the police about Derrick's complaint to the elementary school principal last year?
6. What do you think about the way the police handled this matter?
7. What should you do now that Derrick and Linda are in protective custody?

Part 3—The Parents

Shortly after you get back to your office, you get a very angry phone call from the children's stepfather. Using virtually every obscenity you have ever heard, he calls Derrick a liar, demands that you tell him where the children are, and threatens to beat you up. You hang up and report the matter to the police. Twenty minutes later you get a call from the children's mother. She says that her husband has trashed everything in their trailer and that she has left him and has moved back to her parents' house. She wants to know where her children are and says she wants them back with her. She has done nothing wrong except to marry the wrong man. She is obviously very upset. A few minutes later the natural father of the two children comes into your office, saying that he wants you to have the children placed in his custody. He says he has been trying for some time to get custody of them, because he knew some of what was going on with his ex-wife and her husband. He wants you to give him all the information you can about this incident and about Derrick and Linda in general.

Case Questions

1. What, if anything, can you do about the stepfather's threats? Do you feel in any real danger?
2. What do you tell the children's mother, who was awarded custody of the children at the time of the divorce from their father?
3. How do you deal with the children's stepfather and natural father?
4. What general guidelines should you establish for cases where custody is being contested?
5. How would you prepare if summoned to testify in court on this matter?
6. If in one month's time the mother and her husband are reunited and the courts return the children to them on the provision they attend regular counseling sessions, how will you deal with the situation? What if you learn that the family stopped going to counseling after two sessions?
7. What will you do if the natural father has you summoned to court to testify in a custody hearing?
8. What would you do if the elementary principal were arrested for failure to report child abuse?

SUGGESTED ACTIVITY: Make a directory of all social service agencies in your area. Include names of specific people to contact, as well as the times the agencies are open, any fees for services, the nature of the services provided, and the addresses and phone numbers of the agencies.

PROBLEM 46—TEN SHORT ISSUES: KEEPING SMALL PROBLEMS SMALL

For these issues, assume the role of the superintendent.

A. Eastwick, the smallest town in the district, recently elected Michael C. Browne to the high school board. Mike Browne is well known and well liked in Eastwick. He runs the only garage in the village. The previous Eastwick representative to the high school board was a braggart who was unemployed and probably unemployable. He had been elected last time only because no one else was willing to run. When Mike Browne's name appeared on the ballot, the town was relieved to have a viable alternative, and he won overwhelmingly.

There is just one problem: the man who runs the garage is Michael G. Browne; Michael C. Browne is his son, an 18-year-old high school senior. When Michael C. circulated the petition to have his name placed on the ballot, most people who signed it assumed he was collecting signatures for his father. When it turned out to be the son who won the election, people were surprised, and some thought it was funny. Most of the citizens of Eastwick concluded that Michael C. was a solid, sensible, intelligent kid, a good athlete and an honor roll student who would not disgrace the town as his predecessor had. No one was upset or especially concerned. In the future, however, people would pay more attention to middle initials.

When Michael took his seat with his colleagues on the board, he created a mild sensation. However, he was 18, a resident of Eastwick, and a registered voter. There were no other requirements, and his election was legal.

Case Questions

1. In this case, are there areas of conflict of interest that would prohibit Michael from voting on some issues?
2. As a member of the board, should Michael have the same access to the personnel records of his teachers and administrators as other board members?
3. How would you choose to deal with Michael?

B. The Italian Cultural Club made arrangements many months ago to rent the high school gym, auditorium, and cafeteria for a festival this coming Saturday and Sunday. Because of an incorrect entry in the room utilization log, the assistant high school principal agreed two weeks ago to rent the auditorium to the Republican County Committee for a conference this coming Saturday afternoon and evening. The principal has phoned you to say that the double booking has just been discovered and to ask what should be done.

Case Questions

1. Under what conditions should school facilities be rented to partisan political groups?
2. Which group should get the use of the facility this weekend?
3. What instructions will you give the principal?
4. How will you deal with the two groups?

C. Marcia Talcott has been a fourth-grade teacher in your system for 22 years. She has an excellent reputation and has been absent a total of 4 days in all that time. She has asked to take a personal day two weeks from Friday so that she can fly to her son's wedding, to be held the following day. Her principal refuses to allow her to take the personal day, because it is the Friday before a school vacation and therefore, according to contract, cannot be taken as a personal day. Mrs. Talcott is very upset and has appealed to you.

Case Questions

1. How do you respond to Mrs. Talcott?
2. How will you deal with her principal?
3. If you grant Mrs. Talcott the personal day, will you be setting a precedent that will void the contract provision?

D.   You are at a meeting for superintendents in the state capital. You receive an urgent call from your business manager. The state aid check that was due today has not arrived. Today the note on the high school renovations comes due, and the business manager was counting on the state aid check to pay off the note.

You phone the state comptroller's office and, after some time, manage to get through. A secretary tells you that the state aid checks are to be mailed out this afternoon. You tell her that they were due to arrive today, not to be mailed today. She informs you that the comptroller said that, by keeping the checks until this afternoon, the state could collect considerable interest, since this is a Friday before a long weekend. You remind her that the disbursement of state aid is not a discretionary matter, but rather is set by state law. She says that before you can take any legal action, the money will be in your hands. You demand to speak with the controller. The secretary refuses and hangs up.

After taking 10 deep breaths, you reason that you have enough in your personal account to cover the note if necessary. The state comptroller's office is one block away, and you could go there and demand that they hand over the check immediately. There is a branch of the bank your district uses, which you also use for your personal needs, right across the street. Virtually every superintendent in the state is at the meeting, and they are all affected by the comptroller's action. Mobilization might be easily effected.

Case Questions

1. What consequences are likely if you lend the district your personal funds and repay yourself when the check comes in?
2. What outcome is likely if you go to the comptroller's office and demand the check?
3. What is likely to happen if your district defaults?
4. What would be gained by mobilizing the superintendents?
5. What will you do?

E.   The principal of one of the larger elementary schools has come down with pneumonia and will be out for several weeks at least. She is nearing retirement age. There is a chance that if she does not regain her health quickly or completely, she may elect early retirement, since she has more than the required number of years of service. One of the two assistant high school principals immediately indicates that he is willing to take the post on an interim basis. It is no secret that he has begun looking for a principalship. Your assistant superintendent is an experienced principal, and there are two retired principals in the area who may be willing to take on a short-term assignment.

Case Questions

1. Which option seems to be the most viable immediately? Why?
2. Are there circumstances under which one of the other options would be more attractive? If so, what are they?

F. Angus Williams moved into Eastwick last summer. He rents a two-room apartment above the store and has led a quiet life. No one knows much about him. Today the Eastwick School Board received a bill from a residential facility for severely handicapped children. The bill is larger than the entire Eastwick annual budget. Angus Williams is the father and guardian of the five handicapped children, and according to state child welfare regulations, Eastwick is responsible for the educational portion of their placement. This news comes as an absolute shock to the community.

Case Questions

1. What steps can you take immediately to deal with this bill?
2. Will Eastwick continue to be liable for this expense as long as Angus Williams lives in town or until the children reach the age of 22?
3. Does Eastwick have any options in this matter?

G. Irene Fenwick and Dawn Griffin were made elementary principals last summer. They have both been in the district for many years, are about the same age, and have buildings of nearly the same size. That is where the similarities end. Irene Fenwick calls you nearly every day to tell you the details of everything going on in her school. Dawn Griffin almost never tells you anything, and on three occasions you have learned at board meetings of incidents you should have known about in advance. You have spoken to both principals, but they continue to revert to their established patterns.

Case Questions

1. How can you establish guidelines so that your administrators will know how much information to give you?
2. What will those guidelines be?
3. What steps will you take to deal with these particular administrators?
4. Is there a problem here greater than a misunderstanding about the amount of information that is appropriate?

H.   Jim Allen is the varsity boy's basketball coach and a high school science teacher. During games, he chews tobacco and spits the juice into a plastic cup he carries around. Some of his players have begun chewing tobacco, too. Several people, including two members of the school board, have complained about his habit. You spoke to his principal, and the principal told Jim to stop, at least in public. Jim tried being more discreet, but it was obvious that he was still chewing. His principal ordered him to stop completely, and Jim filed a grievance on the grounds that there is no rule against chewing tobacco, only against smoking. Furthermore, preventing his chewing is a change of working conditions and therefore a contract violation. The principal heard the grievance and denied it. The matter has been appealed to you.

Concurrently, as a result of Jim's action, the chairperson of the school board has asked you to put on the next agenda a change in the wording of the rules. The new wording would prohibit all tobacco use on school grounds, not just smoking.

Case Questions

1. Does Jim have grounds for his grievance?
2. How will you handle the matter?
3. If the chairperson's proposed rule change passes, will it affect the matter being grieved?
4. Has the principal handled this situation well? Might anything more have been done before the matter came back to you?
5. Do teachers who act as coaches under a side agreement have the same contractual rights when coaching as they do when functioning as teachers?

I.   Philip Newton is a high school junior. His principal suspended him for bringing a visiting friend to school without getting permission from the office. One of the members of the elementary school board in the town where Philip resides has just called you. He wants you to ask the high school principal to reverse his decision regarding Philip's suspension. He says Philip is a good kid who does seasonal work on the board member's farm. The visitor is a good kid, too, and used to live in the area before his family moved away. Perhaps Philip should have gotten permission from the office before bringing in a visitor, but a 5-day suspension is rather a severe punishment for such a minor offense.

Case Questions

1. Do you think the principal overreacted, based on what you have been told? What additional information, if any, would be useful?
2. Is it appropriate for an elementary school board member to contact you concerning a high school matter? How do you respond? Would it make a difference if the man were a member of the high school board?
3. What, if anything, will you say to the high school principal about this matter?

4. How will your handling of this situation reflect on the chain of command?

5. How can you teach board members what is appropriate and inappropriate behavior on their part?

J. Your secretary has come to you with a four-page proposal for the color coding of memos. In her plan she would photocopy every memo on colored paper according to subject, using gradations of each color to indicate which audience the memo addressed. The plan would require four shades each of six different colors. You have not seen any problem with memos. You feel that the color coding would only be confusing and would be an unnecessary expense. It is obvious that she has put a good deal of thought into this matter and that it is important to her.

Case Questions

1. How will you deal with the matter?

2. Do you suspect that there is some underlying problem that has generated this proposal? If so, what types of problems should you be looking for?

3. What do you do in general with issues that seem petty to you but seem important to others?

SUGGESTED ACTIVITY: Rank the 10 issues described in this problem in order of probable impact and importance.

PROBLEM 47—THE RENOVATION: ACCOMPLISHING GOALS

For this problem, assume the role of the business manager.

Part 1—School Versus Museum

Centerville School is the second largest school in the district, with slightly more than 300 students. It was built in 1874 and was designated a historic landmark 15 years ago. It is a three-story, red wood-frame building that dominates the north end of the village. It was originally built as a school for grades 1–12, and it served in that capacity until the present regional junior-senior high school was built in 1976.

Over the years many changes have taken place in the structure. In 1927 a gym was added. To save money, the citizens of Centerville had a 3-day gym-building party, in which the men of the town worked to build the addition. Just before the first basketball game was to be played in the new gym, the roof partially collapsed. Rather than cancel or postpone the game, the coach and the team's fathers put a telephone pole near the middle of the basketball court to support the weakened roof. The game was played as scheduled. That stopgap measure stayed in place until 1963, when the roof was finally repaired as part of another renovation. The place where the pole was can still be seen on the gym floor.

The third floor, which used to serve as the high school part of the building, can no longer be used for any purpose except storage, because there is only one means of access. The state has repeatedly tried to force Centerville to build a new school. When inspectors cited more than 100 major building code violations, Centerville fought the state and eventually won their case in court.

Every time the fire bell sounds, many people in town, including the superintendent, hope that it is for Centerville School. The designation as a historic landmark makes renovations even more difficult to accomplish. Last week the sewer pipes that run across the ceiling of the food storage area burst and effectively ended the school's hot lunch program.

The superintendent has ordered you to compile an extensive report on what it would take to bring the building up to code in all areas and make it an educationally sound environment. The underlying aim is to show the people of Centerville that what might have been good enough for their grandparents is no longer good enough for their children and that the only reasonable thing to do is to turn the present building into a museum or cultural center and to build a new school. You are to work with all the agencies that would have to approve the renovations, get cost estimates on all work that needs to be done, find out what aid might be forthcoming from the state, and determine what the renovations would do to local property taxes. You are also supposed to find out what building a new school would cost Centerville taxpayers.

Case Questions

1. Where will you begin?
2. How will you find out which agencies must approve the renovations?
3. How will you find out what renovations are needed to bring the building up to code in all areas?
4. What does it mean to make a building an educationally sound environment?
5. How will you estimate the cost to local taxpayers of making all the renovations needed?
6. How do you find out what it would cost the citizens of Centerville to build a new elementary school for 300+ students?
7. How much time and what resources are you going to need to prepare such a report?
8. The superintendent has an obvious unstated goal. Will you purposely structure your investigation in such a way as to ensure that the local cost of renovating the present building would be far greater than the cost of building a new building? What ethics are involved here? What if your children went to Centerville School?
9. Will you involve the faculty and the principal of the school in writing your report?
10. Do you anticipate that your report will contain anything other than a cost analysis?

Part 2—You Roll Up Your Sleeves

You make arrangements to meet the Centerville principal in the school on a Saturday morning to make a thorough inspection of the building. What you find is incredible. There are at least four different sets of electrical wiring; there are pipes for gas lights; there are at least six roofs, one on top of the other; there are rope ladders meant to be used in case of fire; and the entire third floor is jammed with junk.

Among the junk, you find whole sets of textbooks, some of which were printed in the 19th century; ancient sports equipment; old and broken desks and chairs; flags made before Arizona and Oklahoma were added to the Union; old sports-team uniforms; lighting and plumbing fixtures of a dozen different eras; broken big-screen black-and-white televisions; globes that still show the British, German, Russian, and Ottoman Empires; and debris of every description. Some of it is interesting, and you suggest that the best-preserved examples of each type of item might be cleaned and placed in cases to show Centerville's past. You tell the principal, however, that the vast bulk of what has been stored should simply be thrown away.

The more you uncover, the more fascinated you become with the notion of turning the building into a museum. Just with what you are finding, you could probably set up each classroom to represent a typical classroom of a different era. You could have mannequins dressed in period clothing to represent a teacher, a boy, and a girl of a specific decade. The principal joins in your enthusiasm. It might be possible to find grant money and raise funds to restore the building and open it as a school museum. That might bring tourist dollars to the village, preserve the look of the village, and make a new school more palatable to the residents. Rather than deliver a message involving only dollars and cents, you could point out the possibilities of really preserving the past while providing for the future.

You immediately go to the president of the local historical society and tell her what you have found. You relate the ideas you have generated with the principal. She is instantly intrigued with the idea. She calls some of the people in the society and tells them to meet her at the school as soon as possible. In a half hour 12 people are poring over the contents of the third floor. They begin cataloging items and dating them. Suddenly you realize you have begun something that may rapidly spin out of your control and take you far away from your original purpose.

Case Questions

1. What is your assessment of what has taken place?
2. Will pursuit of the museum idea take you away from your goal of providing a sound educational environment for the children of Centerville?
3. Can you undo what has happened? Should you?
4. What should you tell the superintendent? How will you present it?
5. Has your role now changed? Have your goals?
6. Do you think the present enthusiasm will lead to anything, or is it more likely that it will simply fade?
7. What will you do next?

SUGGESTED ACTIVITY: Prepare a one-page report for the superintendent and the board, advocating turning the school into a museum and building a new school.

PROBLEM 48—THE RED DEVILS: TRADITION VERSUS RELIGION

For this problem, assume the role of the superintendent.

Part 1—The First Two Controversies

Elinor Fowler and three other women from the Church of the Rock have come to see you to give you a petition signed by most of the members of their fundamentalist church. The petition says that they can no longer tolerate having their public high school have a mascot with negative religious symbolism. They say that by having the devil as a mascot either you are saying that the forces of evil at work in the world are mythical, that sin doesn't exist, and that the concept is trite, or you are encouraging devil worship. There is a large red devil on the football, basketball, and baseball scoreboards; in the middle of the gym floor; and on all yearbooks, school sweatshirts, and so on. To make matters worse, you have someone dressed in a red devil costume leading cheers. The women realize the high school mascot was selected long before you came, but they say that, in an age when prayer is banned in schools, such a mascot can no longer be tolerated. Unless you work to have the mascot changed, they will take the matter to court.

A few days later, Heather Wheaton comes into your office with her fifth-grade son's arithmetic workbook. She turns to page 83 and asks you to look at it. You see a page of long division problems. She says that is what you are supposed to see, but she says that the subtle message is clearly there. In the upper right-hand corner is a wizard with a magic wand and a pointy hat with runes on it. Below the figure are the words, "Are you a math wizard?" Mrs. Wheaton says that a few years ago she would have thought nothing of the figure. Now she has had her eyes opened. There is a conspiracy afoot to disparage and undermine Christian values and to lead the young into cults or militant secularism. She says that it is no accident that such characters appear in games, on television, and in movies and videos. There is very little she can do about those except refuse to allow her son to see such things and write letters of protest. She does not, however, have to permit her tax dollars to be spent on distributing such subtle reinforcers to the district's children.

You see that the workbook has been written in and is obviously being consumed. You take a pair of scissors out of your desk and cut off the offending corner of page 83. Mrs. Wheaton responds by saying that you may have sanitized her son's workbook but what about all the other workbooks? In addition, you have still paid the publisher that included the offensive picture. She wants you to stop ordering any materials from that company.

Case Questions

1. How do you respond to Elinor Fowler and her group?
2. How do you respond to Heather Wheaton?

3. Do you consider either or both of these complaints reasonable?

4. Are schools in various ways subtly attacking traditional values and beliefs?

5. Will you bring these concerns to the school board? If so, what do you anticipate their response will be?

Part 2—More Issues Arise

The local newspaper received a letter from Mrs. Wheaton and several letters from members of the Church of the Rock concerning the issues they had brought to your attention. The paper printed some of the letters, and in the Sunday edition of the largest newspaper in your part of the state, there was an editorial prompted by the letters in the local paper. The editorial stated the view that the courts had gone to extremes in forcing the secularization of society and were now attacking organized religion on all fronts, including the schools.

You have started getting more and more calls at home and in your office about the issues of separation of church and state and forced secularization. The calls include many from board members.

One of the board members, Cynthia Ryan, comes to your office. She says that she feels that the questions of the high school mascot and the math wizard are simply silly, and she sympathizes with you about having to deal with such issues. She has a daughter who is a junior in high school, however, and she does have some serious concerns about what is being taught in several areas. She says that, because there seems to be ongoing erosion of the family structure in American society, schools seem to be taking on an ever greater parenting role. She says her family is intact and is perfectly capable of dealing with sensitive issues.

Mrs. Ryan is disturbed that the school is telling her daughter that all philosophical, moral, and religious positions are equally valid. She objects to discussions that conclude by saying that suicide, euthanasia, abortion, ethics, and social behavior and responsibility are all matters of personal choice. She does not condemn monogamous homosexual relationships among adults, but she feels that by handing out condoms, approving all sorts of life-styles, and talking about controlling the spread of AIDS, schools send teenagers the message they want to hear: it is OK to have sex, as long as your partner is willing. She says adolescents are not ready for the complications and responsibilities that sexual relations engender. She points out that in national surveys only 8% of the teenagers who reported having sex reported using condoms.

Mrs. Ryan goes on to say that, even if you accept moral relativity as a standard, you must have the maturity to make responsible decisions and that adolescents lack that level of responsibility. She says that, by negating moral absolutes and substituting values clarification, schools have contributed significantly to American moral decay. The greater parenting role schools take on, the less responsibility children's parents feel. Let schools go back to providing the academic foundation, and let the parents raise the children.

Case Questions

1. What do you think of Mrs. Ryan's statements?

2. Is there reason to believe that schools have overstepped their bounds?

3. How do you respond to Mrs. Ryan?

4. Is there any action you can or should take?

Part 3—The Church of the Rock Becomes Militant

It has been a few weeks since Elinor Fowler and her group came to see you. She phones and asks if you have taken any steps to change the high school mascot. You have just begun to state your position when she cuts you off, saying she thought not, and hangs up. That night the football and baseball scoreboard depictions of red devils are covered over with spray paint. The gym is broken into, tar is poured over the red devil in the middle of the floor, and the red devil on the basketball scoreboard is painted over. The paint can be removed with minimal damage to the scoreboards, but the gym floor is ruined. The entire gym floor will have to be refinished. The refinishing will prevent use of the facility for some time and will be very expensive.

Case Questions

1. How do you respond?

2. What do you anticipate will happen from this point?

3. What types of responses can you anticipate from the board?

4. What will you do about the high school's physical education and sports programs?

5. Is there any way to de-escalate this situation?

SUGGESTED ACTIVITY: Write a one-page paper stating, first, whether public education has established standards that undermine parental authority and traditional religious and moral principles and, second, whether establishing such standards is appropriate for a public school.

PROBLEM 49—THE MALE CHAUVINIST: DEALING WITH SEXISM

For this problem, assume the role of the superintendent.

Part 1—Boys Just Want to Have Fun

Donna Wusterbarth is an assistant principal at the high school. This is her third year on staff. One of her concerns is that there is low female enrollment in the upper-level math and science courses. She has put together a proposal to recognize International Women's Day this year by having an assembly that will highlight the contributions made by women in math and science. She also intends to invite women working in those areas to address the students. Ms. Wusterbarth estimates that the whole program will take one class period. She wants to hold the assembly sixth period because so many programs have already disrupted the seventh period, which is the last. Her intention is that any female student who wants to remain after the assembly and speak to the math- and science-oriented professionals will be allowed to do so. The principal has approved this plan.

Bruce Sanger is a veteran teacher of 27 years. He is the head of the math department and an assistant football coach. He is also an outspoken and blunt critic of the women's movement. He is obnoxious and has alienated himself from a large portion of the faculty. If he were nontenured, you would seriously consider recommending that his contract not be renewed. Bruce's performance is such that you would never be able to prove the grounds his status requires for nonrenewal. He does have a strong following among a few male teachers, most of the other coaches, and the football players.

You have not accepted female student teachers in math because of Bruce's attitude. You are not eager to accept male student teachers into that department for the same reason. There is only one woman in the math department. She has a strong personality and is able to coexist with Bruce. They ignore each other as much as possible.

Stuart and Arthur Grant, 16 and 17 respectively, are brothers and football players. Their best friend is Harry Klein, also a football player. The three boys have been getting away with all sorts of stunts for years because they are genuinely funny and have winning personalities. Bruce sees an opportunity to use the three students to show what he thinks of International Women's Day.

It is traditional for a student to read the end-of-the-day announcements near the close of seventh period. Marc Sunderland is scheduled to read the announcements on International Women's Day. Bruce intimidates Marc into having Harry take his place and writes a message to substitute for the legitimate announcements. Bruce's message is a sarcastic indictment of feminism, ending with a ribald remark about "what women really want." Stuart and Arthur, both of whom have passes issued by Bruce, enter the auditorium as soon as Harry begins his announcement. They are heavily made up and dressed to look like crude caricatures of women. They do their best to disrupt the discussion that is still going on between the speakers and several female students. The school day ends in chaos.

The principal immediately suspends Stuart, Arthur, and Harry for 5 days, asks you to suspend them for 5 more, and asks what should be done about Bruce. The reaction to Bruce's stunt is volatile and immediate. Virtually the entire faculty condemns what he has done, as do most of the students. Word is spreading fast. You can safely assume that the community will soon become involved.

Case Questions

1. Do you think Donna Wusterbarth's plan for acknowledging International Women's Day was appropriate?
2. Do you feel the principal acted appropriately by suspending the three boys? What will you do with them?
3. What do you plan to advise the principal to do about Bruce Sanger?
4. What do you foresee happening?

5. Can you do anything to minimize the disruption this incident will probably cause?

6. How do you plan to present this incident to the board? The press?

Part 2—The Board Acts

The next several days are overwhelmed by the controversy over Bruce Sanger's actions. Opinions differ greatly about what should be done concerning the three boys. They range from pardoning them because the sole responsibility should be Coach Sanger's to expelling them. A few people, including one board member, say that the best thing to do is treat the whole thing as if it were a joke and to keep Bruce Sanger under close scrutiny.

Bruce Sanger's story evolves considerably during those days. Right after the incident, he says that he meant the whole thing as a joke designed to keep people from taking themselves too seriously. He claims that he was just having a little harmless fun and everyone is overreacting. But when his principal asks him to apologize publicly, Bruce refuses, saying that he was lodging a protest against extreme sexism and antimale propaganda. He then protests that the question-and-answer period after the assembly should never have been limited to female students. He goes on to say that affirmative action is keeping countless white males from positions for which they are better qualified than the applicants who are hired, and that this abuse of the civil rights of the white male minority must be terminated immediately. He claims his actions championed true gender equity, were a legitimate form of protest, and were therefore protected by the First Amendment.

Bruce's statements anger many of his colleagues on the faculty. They seem to feel that his statements concerning the erosion of male civil rights are a transparent ploy and that the mention of race is superfluous, since the matter never came up before he threw it in to complicate the situation and confuse the issue. It is clear to them that this is one of his negative and nasty chauvinistic digs, and everyone is tired of hearing them.

The principal has already written a letter of reprimand to be placed in Bruce's file, and the board wants to suspend him for 2 weeks without pay and fine him $2,000.

Case Questions

1. What action will you recommend to the board?

2. Does Bruce Sanger's refusal to apologize constitute insubordination?

3. How do you respond to Bruce Sanger's claim that he was protesting the erosion of the civil rights of white males?

4. If the board fines and suspends Bruce, does he have any grounds for an injunction to prevent the penalties from going into effect?

5. If he does take the matter to court, how will you prepare to respond?

6. How do you feel this matter will eventually be resolved?

SUGGESTED ACTIVITY: Describe on paper how you would decide how far to pursue an issue such as the one presented in this case.

PROBLEM 50—STANDARDIZED TEST SCORES: A POTENTIAL SCANDAL

For this problem, assume the role of the director of pupil personnel services.

Part 1—Artificial Success

For the past several years, the results of the standardized tests for St. Stephen Elementary School have been considerably higher than the test results for the other elementary schools in the district. You are the district's test coordinator and have always found that fact curious. The students from St. Stephen's do not seem to do any better than students from the other schools in the district when they get to high school. This year you decide to investigate the matter more closely.

You begin by speaking to St. Stephen's principal, Dana Winters. You are told that the scores went up after the school started taking a week to prepare the students for the exam. The teachers know that the tests cover specific areas, and they simply review the areas included on the tests. They also review the testing format and have the students take sample tests similar to the ones they will be given. The principal says that tests should measure students' academic achievement, not their level of test anxiety or test-taking ability.

Dana proudly shows you the test preparation materials the teachers use. For each grade there are thick compilations of questions in the same categories as those on the exam: math computation, vocabulary, spelling, math concepts, and so on. There are also answer sheets that correspond to the ones used on the actual exam. You ask if you can borrow the materials to look them over more closely in your office. Dana hesitates, but she agrees.

When you get back to your office, you read through the questions in the test preparation materials. They seem very reasonable. Then you get out a copy of the actual test corresponding to the preparation materials you are reviewing. About every third question in the preparation materials corresponds exactly to a question on the test. Your district owns the testing materials, and you have two sets of question booklets, Form A and Form B. You used Form B this year, but you find a copy of the Form A test. About a third of the questions on the test preparation materials come directly from the alternative form.

Case Questions

1. What will you do?
2. What will you say to the superintendent?
3. What additional information, if any, do you need?
4. What are the legal, moral, and ethical issues here?

5. Do you believe the teachers at St. Stephen are involved in a conspiracy to cheat on the tests?

6. For years the local press and the community have commended St. Stephen for its test results. What will happen if this matter is discovered?

7. The test results are used to place students in the proper tracks when they get to seventh grade. A disproportionate number of students from St. Stephen are in the higher tracks. What, if anything, will you do about that matter?

Part 2—The Story Is Leaked

It has taken hours, but you have gone through all levels of the test preparation materials Dana gave you and all levels of both forms of the actual tests, highlighting all the questions on the preparation materials that duplicate actual test questions. The ratio has remained the same: one-third of the questions come from each form of the test, and the remaining one-third come from neither.

You take the fifth-grade materials in to show the superintendent, leaving the remainder on your desk. The superintendent knew about the week of test preparation and had even commended Dana for it. The superintendent did not know about the duplication of the actual test questions. The disclosure obviously would have many ramifications, and the two of you discuss how to handle the situation for some time. Before you come to any conclusions, the superintendent realizes that it is time to eat a quick supper and go to a school board meeting at Eastwick. You agree to consider the matter and decide on an approach the next day.

When you get home, you discuss the matter with your spouse, giving all details of the discussion between the superintendent and you. The next day is Friday, and the superintendent is out with a stomach virus. The question of the test preparation must wait. There does not seem to be any pressing need for immediate action. The tests for this year have already been completed, and the results distributed. Your discussion will have to wait until Monday.

On Monday morning you are greeted by headlines in the local newspaper that read, "Standardized Tests Rigged at St. Stephen Elementary School". You have not even finished reading the article when the superintendent calls to ask who you told about the test situation. During the course of the conversation, it becomes apparent that neither of you said anything about this situation to anyone except your spouses. The highlighted test preparation materials and the tests themselves are still on top of the worktable in your office, except for the fifth-grade materials, which are on the superintendent's desk.

You search your memory to make sure that you did not mention the matter to anyone except your spouse. The superintendent does the same. Both of you also question your spouses. All four of you conclude that you have told no one or even made hints about the matter. The other people who might have known about the tests were the business manager, the assistant superintendent, the secretaries, and the custodian. The custodian comes in at night for a few hours and is an unlikely suspect.

The information in the newspaper is accurate and fairly detailed. It strongly suggests the possibility of a leak in the central office.

Case Questions

1. Now that the news is public, how will you handle the question of St. Stephen's test preparation? How can you carry on your internal investigation?

2. What criteria are you going to use to place St. Stephen's sixth graders in the junior-senior high school next year?

3. What measures will you take to deal with the faculty and principal of St. Stephen?

4. How will you protect your own reputation?

5. What will you say to the press?

6. How will you investigate the question of who leaked the information to the newspaper?

7. Who had anything to gain by disclosing the information at this time?

8. If you find out who told the press, what will you do?

9. What do you imagine is likely to happen now?

10. What moral and ethical questions do you now face?

SUGGESTED ACTIVITY: Write out the steps you would take to defend your professional reputation if caught in this situation.

CHAPTER SUMMARY

Rural school systems, such as the one in this chapter, have been largely overlooked by many researchers. As a consequence, less thought and attention is paid to them than to urban or suburban systems. Texts and supplies are developed for the urban-suburban population, as are teaching strategies, state regulations, state aid formulas, and most curricula. Change often comes last to rural districts, and much of the change is designed to meet nonrural needs.

In rural systems, the schools are often a focus of a community's social life. Administrators and teachers in such settings may be among the best-paid and best-educated members of the community, and they are scrutinized more than in other settings.

Educators in rural systems must be generalists. Some elementary teachers may teach split-grade classes. Some secondary teachers may teach more than one discipline, and all must teach at several different levels. That means a much greater variety of preparation. It is also probable that many teachers will not have colleagues on site who teach at the same grade level or in the same discipline.

In some larger systems, political patronage contributes to the creation of a very large, often awkward, sometimes effete, and very compartmentalized bureaucracy. Rural central offices are frequently understaffed, and the administrators must constantly shift functions. Communication among central office personnel is essential if the district is to function at all.

Additional stress exists in districts where the superintendent must deal with multiple school boards instead of one central board. Separate boards mean that the number of meetings is multiplied and central office staff must adjust to the expectations, personalities, and demands of each different board. Every board and each of its members may want to deal directly with the superintendent, or the board members may prefer dealing with one of the other central office administrators and avoiding the superintendent. In districts with multiple boards, there are always some board members who do not support the superintendent, and consensus across all boards is very difficult, if not impossible, to achieve.

For the small schools that have a head teacher or a teaching principal, the central office staff must serve as the de facto chief building administrator. Thus, the smaller elementary schools will receive a disproportionately large amount of time and attention from central office personnel, although the bulk of the money to run the central office comes from the larger towns in the district. That fact can cause friction, as can the question of proportional representation on the high school and vocational school boards.

It is impossible for superintendents not to become involved in local political activity, because so much of local politics revolves around the schools. It is vital for the central office staff to remain neutral on as many issues as possible, because the power of the office and the energy of the superintendent must be reserved for those occasions when issues that have a real impact on education are being debated.

Once a disagreement has clearly been lost, it is wise for administrators to concede gracefully, unless the outcome is so serious that they cannot in good faith comply with it. There will be other issues to be won, and the players will remain the same. Central office administrators must be sensitive to the ever-changing nature of their support. They will have board members and community leaders who generally support them but who are occasionally on the opposite side of an argument. If the administration alienates those people, the central office will erode its power base and eventually lose its ability to lead. It is very tempting to enter into private understandings with key people. The danger is that administrators may compromise their integrity and principles. There are times at which an administrator might want to consider whether it is time to move on.

Because rural administrators work in such isolation, often the only people they can freely and safely discuss professional problems with are their counterparts in other systems. Opportunities to meet with colleagues are important because professionals must have healthy outlets to reduce stress and shed burdens on a regular basis.

FINAL SUGGESTED ACTIVITY: Review the decisions you have made throughout this book. Decide what you have learned about yourself and whether you would now revise some of the earlier decisions you made. Consider whether you encountered any surprises, validated what you already knew, or evolved in any way.

SUMMARY QUESTIONS

1. As superintendent, how would you plan to work with so many different school boards?

2. How would you delegate responsibility to the four central office administrators?

3. Would you function significantly differently as the superintendent of a regional rural district than as the superintendent of a town school district with the same number of students? If so, how?

4. If you were superintendent of Marsden North, would you try to consolidate your smaller schools? If so, how and under what circumstances? If not, why not? What would be the advantages and disadvantages of consolidating?

5. What criteria would you use to evaluate the four central office administrators, the building administrators, and the head teachers?

6. How would you go about planning in-service workshops for the professional staff of Marsden North?

7. What services, if any, would you provide for the smaller schools that you would not provide for the larger ones?

8. How would you deal with the local media? Local civic groups? Would your relationships with such organizations be any different if you were superintendent than if you were a principal?

9. Would you set up administrative teams? If so, how would they function?

10. Where would you draw the boundaries of your professional responsibilities?

SUGGESTED READING

Alexander, K. (1980). *School law.* St. Paul, MN: West.

Allen, D. W. (1992). *Schools for a new century: A conservative approach to radical school reform.* Westport, CT: Praeger.

Castetter, W. (1986). *The personnel function in educational administration* (4th ed.). New York: Macmillan.

Cooper, B. S. (Ed.). (1992). *Labor relations in education: An international perspective.* Westport, CT: Greenwood Press.

Greenhalgh, J. (1978). *Practitioner's guide to school business management.* Boston, MA: Allyn & Bacon.

Guthrie, J.. & Reed, R. (1986). *Educational administration and policy.* Englewood Cliffs, NJ: Prentice-Hall.

Frost, P. J., Moore, L. F., Lousi, M. R., Lundberg, C. C., and Martin, J. (1985). *Organizational culture.* Beverly Hills, CA: Sage.

Hanson, E. (1985). *Educational administration and organizational behavior* (2nd ed.). Boston, MA: Allyn & Bacon.

Hess, A. G. (Ed.). (1992). *Empowering teachers and parents: School restructuring through the eyes of anthropologists.* Westport, CT: Bergin & Garvey.

Hoy, W. K., & Miskel, C. G. (1991). *Educational administration: Theory, research and practice* (4th ed.). New York: McGraw-Hill.

Huse, E. F., & Cummings, T. G. (1985). *Organizational development and change* (3rd ed.). St. Paul, MN: West.

Lankard, B. A. (1987). *Accepting responsibility.* Columbus, OH: National Center for Research in Vocational Education, Ohio State University.

Levine, M. (1988). *Effective problem solving.* Englewood Cliffs, NJ: Prentice-Hall.

Lortie, D. (1975). *The semi-professions and their organization.* New York: Free Press.

McCall, J. B., & Cousins, J. (1990). *Communication problem solving: The language of effective management.* New York: Wiley.

Mintzberg, H. (1989). *Mintzberg on Management.* New York: The Free Press.

Olafson, F. A. (1973). *Ethics and twentieth century thought.* Englewood Cliffs, NJ: Prentice-Hall.

O'Reilly, R. C., & Green, E. T. (1992). *School law for the 1990s: A handbook.* Westport, CT: Greenwood.

Ornstein, A. C., & Hunkins, F. P. (1992). *Curriculum: Foundations, principles and issues.* Boston, MA: Allyn & Bacon.

Owens, R. G. (1970). *Organizational behavior in schools.* Englewood Cliffs, NJ: Prentice-Hall.

Pajak, E. (1989). *The central office supervisor of curriculum and instruction.* Boston, MA: Allyn & Bacon.

Pennings, J. M., & Assoc. (1985). *Organizational strategy and change.* San Francisco, CA: Jossey-Bass.

Plunkett, L. C., & Hale, G. A. (1982). *The proactive manager: The complete book of problem solving and decision making.* New York: Wiley-Interscience.

Pruitt, D. G., & Rubin, J. Z. (1986). *Social conflict: Escalation, stalemate, and settlement.* New York: Random House.

Rosenhead, J. (Ed.). (1989). *Rational analysis for a problematic world: Problem structuring methods for complexity, uncertainty, and conflict.* New York: Wiley.

Sanderson, M. (1979). *Successful problem management.* New York: Wiley.

Sandole, D. J., & Sandole-Staroste, I. (Eds.). (1987). *Conflict management and problem solving: Interpersonal to international applications.* New York: New York University Press.

Sergiovanni, T. (1989). *Moral leadership: Getting to the heart of school improvement.* San Francisco, CA: Jossey-Bass.

Sergiovanni, T. (1989). *Schooling for tomorrow: Directing reforms to issues that count.* Boston, MA: Allyn & Bacon.

Sybouts, W. (1992). *Planning in school administration: A handbook.* Westport, CT: Greenwood.

Tanner, D., & Tanner, L. (1987). *Supervision in education: Problems and practices.* New York: Macmillan.

Tarr, G. (1973). *The management of problem-solving: Positive results from productive thinking.* New York: Wiley.

Valente, W. D. (1987). *Law in the schools.* New York: Macmillan.

Walker, D. (1990). *Fundamentals of curriculum.* New York: Harcourt Brace Jovanovich.

Webb, L. D., Greer, J. Y., Montello, P. A., & Norton, M. S. (1987). *Personnel administration in education.* Columbus, OH: Merrill.

Wiles, J., & Bondi, J. (1989). *Curriculum development: A guide to practice.* New York: Macmillan.

Yukl, G. (1989). *Leadership in organizations* (2nd ed.). Englewood Cliffs, NJ: Prentice Hall.

Zais, R. (1976). *Curriculum: Principles and foundation.* New York: Harper Collins.

Index

••••••

The following index of the issues presented in the cases in this book is far from exhaustive. There are many ways of looking at and classifying cases. This is simply one of many possible organizations. It classifies cases in ways which might not be apparent from the table of contents, case titles and subtitles, and is different from the classification used in the topic matrix located at the beginning of this book. Some issues such as principal/teacher relations are so all encompassing as to make classifying them redundant. A strong case could be made for claiming that all cases have possible legal implications or affect community relations. The classification below focuses in on the most central issues in each case.

About the Author

......

Robert E. Kirschmann began teaching in New York City in 1968 after completing his bachelors degree at Fordham University. He finished his masters in educational administration at Worcester State College in August 1976. At the University of Oregon, Bob earned a second masters in 1977 and a doctorate in 1980. Both these degrees were in curriculum and instruction. Since 1980 he has been a K–8 principal, a 7–12 principal, a curriculum director, and an assistant superintendent of schools.

Bob is currently an associate professor at the University of Bridgeport where he teaches courses in teacher education and educational management programs. This is his first book.

Bob lives with his wife and two children in Meriden, Connecticut. He focuses his life on his immediate and extended family, close friends, students and colleagues, his Catholic faith, and his duties as a homemaker.